Why Did God Create Man?

Dennis R Dinger

Why Did God Create Man?

ISBN   978-1-365-88932-5

Published by: **C.B. Dinger**
103 Augusta Rd., Clemson, SC 29631
(864) 654-3155
E-mail: dennis@dingerceramics.com

*to all who ever
asked this question . . .*

Contents

Preface

The question, "Why did God create man?" has been one I've pondered for years. I have addressed this subject in other writings, and I have the nagging feeling that I haven't explained it well. So I am addressing it again!

I have no doubts that we are created beings. Evolution simply does not adequately explain the intricate complexities of life! It cannot! As a computer programmer, I know how difficult it is to take into account all possibilities in any task. I once attempted to write a computer program which would accept a raw data signal and then smooth it. Every time I thought I had taken into account all possible variations in the data, a new unanticipated variation would show itself. . . . it was frustratingly complex! . . . and that was just to accept and smooth a simple data stream.

The complexities of the human body give it abilities to handle all manner of difficult circumstances. Our bodies can reproduce, grow, age, handle accidents and disease, perform all normal life functions, etc. Many of these abilities are not functional until needed! All happen without any conscious efforts on our parts! This miraculous design should prove to everyone that man has been designed by a Master Designer and formed by a Master Engineer!

The design of the human body makes my data smoothing problem seem quite trivial! . . . and there's no way random processes can accomplish the intertwined complexities and magnificent functionality of the human body! Creation of such elegance by a superior engineering mind is the only possible answer!

The heavens, the earth, and all life were created by the amazing creativity and ability of the God of the universe!

But why did God make man? Why did He make us like this? Why did He place us here on the earth? There must be a reason!

These are the questions addressed in this book. I think the answers make wonderful sense! Hopefully, my readers will agree with that assessment!

Details of This Book

All Bible quotations in this book are from the King James Version. They are shown in "**bold.**" For *emphasis*, I have used combinations of **bold**, *italics*, and <u>underlines</u>.

I pray that the Lord will edify all who read this study and give each one real excitement and desire to learn the truths of the Bible.

God bless every one who undertakes this study to learn the scriptural answers to, "Why did God create man?"

Dennis R. Dinger
14 March 2017

1

Introduction

Many people throughout history have asked: Why are we here? Why did God create man? Why did God create the earth? Why did God make us like this? If God knew mankind could sin, why didn't He create us so we could **not** sin?

There are simple answers to these questions which we see demonstrated throughout the Bible. The Lord, however, never stated the answers to any of these questions in any single, easy verse. We need to look into the mind of God, the words He uses, and the actions He takes throughout the whole Bible, to identify His reasons. . . . but answers to these questions **are** present in the Bible for all to see!

The Simple Answer to the Main Question

Why did God create man? The simple answer to this fundamental question is that God created man to be a family of His own whom He can love, for whom He can care, and with whom He can fellowship. With these goals in mind, God created the heavens and the earth as a dwelling place for us.

We see God's desire for a people of His own presented over and over again throughout the scriptures. We see evidence of this in the creation of Adam and Eve. We see evidence in God's promises to Abraham, in His words to the children of Israel, and in His words to all mankind at the end of the book of Revelation. Evidences in support of this desire appear throughout the whole of the Bible.

Why does any man and woman want to marry and raise a family? Any reasons we can give in answer to this question are the same reasons God can give for creating mankind!

We are all motivated to have children and raise a family. Should we be surprised to learn that God thinks that way, too?

Before Creating Man, Did God Take Sin Into Account?

Why did God create man with the ability to sin? Why didn't God create man in such a way that sin was not possible? The answers to these questions have to do with God's desire to fellowship with man. We will discuss them as we proceed throughout this study.

We will especially consider statements made by God, which give insight into His thinking! When we break down His words to their simplest parts, God's motives for His actions make wonderful sense!

Many people do not give proper weight to God's words, which express His desire for a people of His own! Of those who believe in Creation, some consider God to be an aloof higher being who matter-of-factly created the world and all life in it. Many don't believe in Creation at all! They suggest humankind evolved from lower forms of life, so no god whatsoever was necessary to produce any forms of life! . . . and yet the evidence shows that God did create; we did **not** evolve from single-celled life; and the God of Creation is a loving God who cares deeply for mankind and for this whole creation!

God's Family

Let us jump ahead to eternity future. All those who believe God, throughout Old and New Testament times, will make up the family of God who will spend eternity in His presence!

Everyone who rejected God in this life, and refused His every offer of help, will get their wish, too. No one will ever be forced to spend any time at all with God!

Free will made this possible. By giving mankind free will, all those who want to be God's people will be, and all those who do not want to be God's people won't be! Everybody can choose for themselves!

The result: God will have a family of people of His own with whom He will spend eternity! His people will include all who want to be His children and members of His family, all who want to spend eternity with Him, all who want to love Him, and all who totally appreciate His every effort on their behalf!

The Structure of This Book

Old Testament Times

To examine God's desire for a people of His own, we will start with Adam and consider many of the leaders of the people with whom God dealt throughout Old Testament times. We will consider leaders who lived in the land of Israel before the major captivities of the children of Israel in Assyria and in Babylonia.

From Abraham's time forward, God dealt with a single family — descendants of Abraham, Isaac, and Jacob, whom we know as *the children of Israel*. As God had Moses repeat numerous times, the children of Israel were God's chosen people — He considered them, "**My people.**" When they were in slavery in Egypt, God sent Moses to rescue them and lead them out through the Red Sea and the wilderness of Sinai. God led them into the promised land under the leadership of Joshua. For a few years, He appointed judges to lead the people.

All of these leaders were supposed to be taking their guidance from the Lord God and setting examples for the people which would teach them to rely on the Lord! During all those years, God wanted the people to look to Him, but both leaders and people continued to turn further and further away from Him!

Of all mankind, the children of Israel had a unique relationship with the Lord God. They had the Lord God of the universe caring for them, protecting them, guiding them, loving them, etc., yet they didn't want His attention! . . . and they certainly didn't appreciate their special relationship to Him! They wanted a king! . . . a human king! Finally, after they totally rejected the Lord God's leadership, He gave them a king!

Again in each case, God wanted the kings to set examples for the people to lead them to the Lord and to encourage them to obey His statutes and commandments. In return, He would be their God.

God led the children of Israel and cared for them through many crises in their lives, for which they gave Him no credit whatsoever! It didn't matter what He did! Over and over again, the children of Israel rejected the Lord God's leadership.

Ultimately, God rejected the children of Israel by casting them out of the land and into slavery to foreign kings.

God's Prophet

Early in the process, when Moses was leading the people, God promised to send "**a Prophet**" unto them who would be like them. This Prophet would speak God's words to them!

When God spoke to Moses up on mount Sinai, with all the dark clouds, lightning, and booming thunder which accompanied God's presence, the people feared God. So they need not fear every time God wanted to speak to them, He promised to send a Prophet!

The Prophet He sent was His Son, Jesus Christ. Having tried to draw the children of Israel to Him through the various leaders of the Old Testament, He sent Jesus to walk, talk, live, and represent the Lord God among them. Jesus is the subject of the whole New Testament.

Near the end of the Old Testament, God told the children of Israel that He was going to make another people, "**which were not My people,**" to be His people. (Hosea 2:23) He was going to offer His love to the Gentiles (and of course still to any individual Jews who were interested.) All those who believed and accepted His love would be His people. This change of emphasis appears in the New Testament.

Why did God begin to offer eternal life to **all** mankind? . . . because Jesus Christ offered Himself for **all** mankind — Jew and Gentile alike! . . . and to **all** who accept His offer, He declares, "**Thou art My people.**" All who accept His offer will say in return, "**Thou art my God.**" (Hosea 2:23)

New Testament Times

The four New Testament Gospels present the life of Jesus Christ and show, in great detail, all of His redemptive work towards mankind. The New Testament epistles explain how all mankind can place their faith in the Son of God, and receive salvation and new life as members of God's family! The book of Acts and the epistles give explanations, and examples of men of God operating under the empowerment of the Holy Spirit.

Throughout the Old Testament, the Lord focused on the children of Israel. In the New Testament, however, the Lord takes His message to **all mankind**. The Jews in the Old Testament had their chance to be His people, and they refused. In the New Testament, the Good News of the Gospel of Jesus Christ is preached to **all** — Jew and Gentile alike! Now, everyone is invited to become children of God!

The Gospel message appeared in the Old Testament, but it was hidden — and it was not made clear until Paul identified it. We do have examples of exceptions in the Old Testament — that is, examples of people who were not children of Israel but who were believers. Ruth, a Moabitess, is such an example, as is Rahab of Jericho. In fact, both Ruth and Rahab (Rachab) appear in the genealogy of Jesus Christ! (Matthew 1:5) . . . but the Lord's main focus during Old Testament times was on the children of Israel! . . . and they rejected Him!

Unlike the Old Testament message, the Good News of the New Testament goes out to "**whosoever will**"! **Everybody** today hears the Good News of Jesus Christ! . . . Jew and Gentile alike!

Our goal throughout this whole study is to show how the Lord God interacted with mankind throughout Old Testament times, how He tried to draw the children of Israel to Him, and how He continues to interact with mankind throughout New Testament times. We especially want to show and explain how the Lord God actually solved the sin problem through the person and work of His Son Jesus Christ!

God did all of this to achieve a people of His own with whom He will spend eternity loving, caring, and fellowshipping!

We ask God's blessing upon all who undertake to study this book, and to study the Bible, to learn: Why did God create man?

So let's begin!

God's Purpose
for Creating Mankind

In the introductory chapter, we stated a simple answer to the question, "Why did God create man?" To reiterate, God placed man on earth to be a people of His Own whom He can love, and with whom He can fellowship. Because God is eternal, His care, love, and fellowship with a family of mankind will extend for all eternity!

This is truly wonderful desire of God towards mankind!

God Placed Adam & Eve in the Garden

The first evidence we see that God wanted to fellowship with mankind is in the garden of Eden.

According to Genesis 1 & 2, God created Adam and Eve; He created the garden of Eden as a paradise on earth; and then He placed the two in it.

What were His stated purposes for mankind? He declared that man should **"have dominion"** over all the earth and over all its creatures. (Genesis 1:26) He told them, **"Be fruitful, and multiply, and replenish the earth, and subdue it: and have dominion over the fish of the sea, and over the fowl of the air, and over every living thing that moveth upon the earth."** (Genesis 1:28) Then, we read, **"And the LORD God took the man, and put him into the garden of Eden to dress it and to keep it."** (Genesis 2:15)

The several stated purposes why God created mankind, put them on the earth, and placed them in the garden are:

- to have dominion over the earth,
- to have dominion over all earth's creatures,
- to be fruitful and multiply,
- to replenish the earth,
- to dress the garden, and
- to keep the garden (that is, to protect it.)

From this, it is quite clear that God created the earth to be a dwelling place for mankind. He created and placed all manner of living creatures and plant life upon the earth. . . . and finally, He created man and woman, and placed them in the garden with these duties to accomplish. All of this defines man's part in the equation!

What Was In It for God?

None of the tasks given to man, however, explains the "Why?" of the creation. What was in it for God?

A Companion for Man

God's stated reason for creating a woman for Adam gives an indication of His thinking regarding fellowship. This reasoning also appears to apply to His own desires.

"And the LORD God said, 'It is not good that the man should be alone; I will make him an help meet for him." (Genesis 2:18)

God believed man should have a companion, and for that reason He created the woman! God understood what it would be like for Adam to go through life without another like him. . . . so God created Eve out of Adam's side. She was a part of him; she was like him; she would complement him; she would be a companion to him; and she would be his wife and mother of his children.

Companions for God???

God's words, **"It is not good that the man should be alone,"** is a simple statement of fact from the Creator God. . . . but this declaration gives us insight into His own thinking. As we know, God created man in His own image and His own likeness. This means that mankind, both Adam and Eve, and all of their descendants, were to be **like** God! . . . and by creating them in His **image**, they would be His representatives on earth.

Since Adam was created to be like God, this suggests that God thought it good for everyone to have someone with whom to fellowship — including Himself. God didn't *need* companions — emphasis on the word *need* — because, as we know, He had His Son, whom we know as Jesus Christ, by His side always.

God the Father and Jesus the Son had fellowshipped with one another for all eternity. . . . but a family of innumerable size who would define Jesus' generation, who would be like God and like the Son, who would represent them on earth, and with whom They could fellowship going forward — appears to have been a very appealing idea to God!

All three parts of the Godhead, God the Father, Jesus the Son, and the Holy Spirit, were involved in the creation of man! They were in total agreement. The word *God* in Genesis 1:26, is a plural noun, as are the pronouns which follow. **"And God said, 'Let us make . . ."** The Godhead were in agreement when they created man to be like them! . . . to represent them on earth! . . . and, of course, with whom they could fellowship.

Fellowship?

What was God doing when we see Him in the garden which He prepared for Adam and Eve? He was looking for them, calling out to them, and wanting to talk to them!

"And they heard the voice of the LORD God walking in the garden in the cool of the day . . ." (Genesis 3:8)

God prepared a paradise on earth (the garden of Eden) in which He placed man (Adam & Eve) and then **"in the cool of the day,"** God took a stroll in the garden. . . . and when He couldn't find the two people, He called out to them: **"And the LORD God called unto Adam, and said unto him, 'Where art thou?' "** (Genesis 3:9) God was looking for them! He wanted to spend time with them — to fellowship with them!

Why do people take strolls in gardens? We do so because it is pleasant! . . . and when we do it in the cool of the day, it is even more pleasant! What makes it even more pleasant than that? It is delightful to take a stroll, and converse with a beloved while together enjoying the beauties of the surroundings!

God expected to find Adam and Eve in the garden when He went for His stroll. What was in it for God? Fellowship! Fellowship with beloved members of His family! Fellowship with those who were like Him! Fellowship with friends!

Which of the creatures on earth were created who could walk, talk, love, reminisce, rejoice, and enjoy all the attributes God gave to Adam? None of the other creatures were like God! None of the other creatures were like Adam! . . . and that led to God's stated reason for creating Eve!

How do we know this? All of the living creatures paraded before Adam, **"but for Adam there was not found an help meet for him."** (Genesis 2:20) Following that parade, God made Eve to be a companion for Adam. She was like him! She was part of him! She was Adam's complement! She would be able to love him, share with him, enjoy his company, celebrate with him, and so on!

So Eve was made to love and fellowship with Adam, and in like manner, it appears that Adam and Eve were created to love and fellowship with God! The evidence in Genesis 1 and 2, suggests this was the case!

Further Evidences

If this conclusion is correct, and God did place mankind on earth to be a people with whom He could fellowship, we should see more evidences of it throughout the whole Bible! . . . and we do!

God's Covenant with Abram

When God spoke to Abram in Genesis 15, He said, **"Fear not, Abram: I am thy shield, and thy exceeding great reward."** (Genesis 15:1)

God was watching over and protecting Abram! That very protection was an **"exceeding great reward"** to Abram and family. God was caring for and protecting the very people with whom He wanted to fellowship!

Then, in Genesis 17, God told Abraham, "**I am the Almighty God; walk before me, and be thou perfect.**" (Genesis 17:1) A few verses later, God said, "**And I will establish My covenant between Me and thee and thy seed after thee in their generations for an everlasting covenant, to be a God unto thee, and to thy seed after thee.**" (Genesis 17:7)

God made an "**everlasting**" covenant with Abraham, and with his descendants, "**to be a God**" unto them! Note again that this covenant was not only to Abraham, but also, "**to thy seed after thee.**"

A little later, God told Abraham, "**And God said, 'Sarah thy wife shall bear thee a son indeed; and thou shalt call his name Isaac: and I will establish My covenant with him for an everlasting covenant, and with his seed after him.'**" (Genesis 17:19) God promised to confirm the covenant He made with Abraham, with Abraham's son Isaac, and with Isaac's seed after him!

We also read that the Lord confirmed the covenant with Jacob, Isaac's son: "**[13]And, behold, the LORD stood above it, and said, 'I am the LORD God of Abraham thy father, and the God of Isaac: the land whereon thou liest, to thee will I give it, and to thy seed; [14]and thy seed shall be as the dust of the earth, and thou shalt spread abroad to the west, and to the east, and to the north, and to the south: and in thee and in thy seed shall all the families of the earth be blessed. [15]And, behold, I am with thee, and will keep thee in all places whither thou goest, and will bring thee again into this land; for I will not leave thee, until I have done that which I have spoken to thee of.'**" (Genesis 28:13-15)

The Lord was promising to care for the descendants of Abraham, to bless them, to make them fruitful, and to give them a great land. The Lord was acting like a Father to His children — the children of Israel — and most especially, they would enjoy being the children of God!

When the children of Israel were slaves in the land of Egypt, God referred to them as "**My people.**" Numerous times God sent Moses to Pharaoh, to repeat His words: "**Let My people go**"!

The children of Israel had become "**My people**" — that is, God's people! . . . whom He loved! They were "**a special people unto Himself.**" We note that the Lord told Moses He chose the children of Israel to be His people: "**because the LORD loved you.**"

"**[6]For thou art an holy people unto the LORD thy God: the LORD thy God hath chosen thee to be a special people unto Himself,** above all people that are upon the face of the earth. [7]The LORD did not set His love upon you, nor choose you, because ye were more in number than any people; for ye were the fewest of all people: [8]but <u>because the LORD loved you</u>, and because He would keep the oath which He had sworn unto your fathers, hath the LORD brought you out with a mighty hand, and redeemed you out of the house of bondmen, from the hand of Pharaoh king of Egypt.

[9]Know therefore that the LORD thy God, He is God, the faithful God, which keepeth covenant and mercy with them that love Him and keep His commandments to a thousand generations." (Deuteronomy 7:6-9)

It is clear that God considered the children of Israel to be His children! They were a special people unto Him! He loved them! He redeemed them! . . . and He was watching over them!

He was keeping His promises which He made to Abraham. Why? He said He "**keepeth covenant and mercy with them that love Him and keep His commandments.**" Abraham's descendants were His people!

God's Stated Purpose

In preparation for rescuing the children of Israel from Egypt, God told Moses to speak these words to the children of Israel:

"**And I will take you to Me for a people, and I will be to you a God: and ye shall know that I am the LORD your God, which bringeth you out from under the burdens of the Egyptians.**" (Exodus 6:7)

God clearly told the people in this verse that they were **His people**, and He was their God! He was going to care for them, and bring them "**out from under the burdens of the Egyptians.**" That is, He was going to rescue them and redeem them from slavery!

God's Purpose Has Not Changed

One might think that with all the sin and rebellion coming from all mankind all over the earth, God could have changed His thinking about mankind over the course of time.

We learn how God still thinks after all these years, however, when we consider the following passage from Revelation 21 (the second last chapter in the whole Bible), in which the Apostle John is describing eternity future:

"And I heard a great voice out of heaven saying, 'Behold, the tabernacle of God is with men, and He will dwell with them, and they shall be His people, and God Himself shall be with them, and be their God.' " (Revelation 21:3)

Even when we look ahead to eternity, which is what John was doing, the "**tabernacle of God . . .**" that is, "the <u>dwelling place</u> of God," ". . . **is with men**"! The dwelling place of God is with men! Even after more than 6000 years of experiences which showed God exactly what He can expect from mankind, God still wants to dwell with men! They will be His people! God Himself will be with them! . . . and God Himself will be their God!

These words in Revelation 21:3 are almost identical to the words in Exodus 6:7. All of the events recorded in the Bible, and all of the years between God's promise to Abraham in Genesis, to the children of Israel in Exodus, and to all mankind in Revelation 21 did not cause God to change His mind. His goal remains the same!

God placed mankind here on earth to be His family — with whom He can fellowship, love, care, bless, etc. . . . and His great desire to spend quality time with mankind has not changed at all throughout all the years of mankind's history!

Throughout the Old Testament, God dealt with the children of Israel. When they rejected Him, He began to deal with Jesus' generation who come from **all** people — Jew and Gentile alike! One day soon, all children of Israel who have rejected God — as a nation — will recognize their mistake and join Jesus' generation! Then, Jesus will gather all of His generation to spend eternity together!

This passage in Revelation 21, describes exactly what we can expect during eternity future in heaven! . . . and God's stated purpose, after more than 6000 years of man on earth, has not changed: **"The tabernacle of God is with men, and He will dwell with them, and they shall be His people, and God Himself shall be with them, and be their God."**

The Creation of Adam

Let's look at the details of the creation of man by God as recorded in Genesis 1 & 2.

"Let Us Make Man"

Here is the main passage describing the creation of man:

"²⁶And God said, 'Let us make man in our image, after our likeness: and let them have dominion over the fish of the sea, and over the fowl of the air, and over the cattle, and over all the earth, and over every creeping thing that creepeth upon the earth.'

²⁷So God created man in His own image, in the image of God created He him; male and female created He them.

²⁸And God blessed them, and God said unto them, 'Be fruitful, and multiply, and replenish the earth, and subdue it: and have dominion over the fish of the sea, and over the fowl of the air, and over every living thing that moveth upon the earth.' " (Genesis 1:26-28)

The second chapter of Genesis takes this a little further:

"⁷And the LORD God formed man of the dust of the ground, and breathed into his nostrils the breath of life; and man became a living soul." (Genesis 2:7)

As mentioned already, all of the words for God and the pronouns which refer to God, are plural forms. This shows that all three Persons of the Triune God had a hand in the creation of man. "And God said . . . Let us . . . our image . . . our likeness . . . So God . . . in the image of

15

God . . . and <u>God</u> blessed them, and <u>God</u> said . . ." This also shows that there was **unity** in the Godhead with respect to the creation of man!

The Triune God proposed the creation of man in verse 26, created man just that way in verse 27, and blessed man in verse 28.

A Living Soul

The additional, important information we learn from Genesis 2:7 is that God made man **"a living soul."** This is the part of man which medical science does not understand and cannot touch. The soul of man is the eternal part of man.

God breathed into man's nostrils **"the breath of life,"** and man became **"a living soul."** Ask anyone about the three fundamental parts of man and most will answer that they are body, soul, and spirit. This verse suggests that man is a living soul, which has a body and a spirit. . . . and God's own order of importance is spirit, soul, and body. (1 Thessalonians 5:23)

Physicians learn to heal the body, but when the soul leaves the body, the man dies. Physicians do not know how to heal the soul, nor do they know how to prevent a soul from leaving the body, nor how to bring a soul back into a dead body.

The soul is the part of man that evolution cannot explain. (We understand even less about the spirit, but that is another issue.) Evolutionists would have us believe that if they managed (somehow) to put together all appropriate parts to form a man, that creation would automatically come to life. Actually, evolutionists say that we evolved into this complex physical form from single-celled life over eons of time!

With regard to any kind of life, evolutionists cannot explain how **life** enters a body. The assumption is that when the physical body is right (that is, when it is complete in all its necessary details), life just automatically appears.

Evolutionists teach that man evolved from single-celled life. Biologists know even less about what gives life to a single-celled creature than they know about the life — the soul — of mankind!

The goal of evolutionists everywhere is to explain how man evolved into this physical form. But no one ever touches the underlying issue of the soul, or the topic of **life** — because no one can explain it! If, by means of evolutionary processes, or by the hand of someone like Dr. Frankenstein, a body with all its necessary parts has been assembled, evolutionists assume it will automatically come to life. They must assume this because they have no other explanation for it!

If life happened automatically like evolutionists suggest, no one would ever die!   Plus Genesis 2:7 would be a lie! Why would God need to make man **"a living soul"** if life in a body is automatic? Form the body and *Voilà*! Life! . . . but it doesn't happen that way!

When a person dies, the body still has all the necessary parts to give that person life! So why do people die? Physicians and evolutionists cannot explain it — other than to say that the body stopped functioning properly. Physicians cannot explain **why** the soul leaves the body. . . . or **how** the soul leaves the body. Evolutionists have no idea, period! Since evolutionists cannot explain life nor death, they ignore it and hope no one notices the gigantic hole in their theory!

Moses presented the two-step creation of man by God. Step 1: God formed man's body; and Step 2: God breathed into the body the breath of life, and man became a living soul! It's a two-step process, and the creation story explains it. Evolution cannot even adequately explain the first step!

Dr. Frankenstein brought his monster to life with an electric shock. Evolutionists believe naturally occurring electrical events somehow completed the necessary evolutionary steps in single-celled creatures. According to evolutionists, when the primordial ooze contained the right compounds in proper relative amounts, and a stray lightning bolt supplied the necessary energy, complex proteins were formed!   Even if this happened, from where did the life come? No one knows!

Complex proteins alone are just complex hydrocarbons. They do not have life. Again, we must ask: From where does the life come?

21st Century medical doctors know how to make muscles twitch by appropriately placed electrical impulses, but they have no idea how to send a soul which has left the body back into the body.

Jesus, however, **does** know how to do that! He raised Lazarus after he was dead for more than three days. In fact, after that amount of time, Lazarus' body had begun to decay. It was no longer whole; it could no longer function properly due to decay! . . . and yet Jesus raised Lazarus to life! He healed Lazarus' body and brought his soul back into it! Medical science cannot do that! They do not know how to do it! . . . and they know they don't know!

When medical doctors use a defibrillator, they use it to shock the heart muscles to start it beating again. They aren't attempting in any way to affect the person's soul with the defibrillator! They are attempting to make the heart muscles twitch! . . . and to start the heart beating again. Defibrillators cause muscles to twitch; their electricity may even stimulate nerve cells; but they have no known effect on the soul!

The soul is the part of man which gives each of us our unique character – our personality. God made Adam a living soul! . . . and then later, He did the same for Eve!

All of the living beings created in Genesis 1 are souls! The same words describe the living creatures as are translated **"living soul"** with respect to man. In Genesis 2:7, the Hebrew for *living soul* is *chay nephesh*. (Strong's) The word *life* in Genesis 1:12, which describes **"the moving creature that hath <u>life</u>"** is the Hebrew *chay nephesh*. (Strong's) The expression **"living creature,"** in Genesis 1:21, which refers to life in the oceans is the Hebrew *chay nephesh*. (Strong's) **"Living creature"** in Genesis 1:24, which refers to animals, is the Hebrew *chay nephesh*. (Strong's) With respect to all creatures wherein there is **"life,"** Genesis 1:30, the word *life* is the Hebrew *nephesh chay*.

Just as medical doctors don't know anything about the living souls of mankind, veterinarians don't know anything about the living souls of animals.

Mankind simply knows nothing about souls! . . . other than that we know we **are** souls! . . . and animals **are** souls! The understanding of the concept of *souls*, however, is well beyond the capabilities of mankind!

The Image and Likeness of God

Genesis 1:26 & 27 both indicate that man was made in **the image of God**. Genesis 1:26 also indicates man was made in **the likeness of God**.

The Image of God

An *image* implies *representation* of the one whom the object's likeness reflects. The word *image* means "a representative *figure*." (Strong's)

The "**molten calf,**" Aaron made for the people was an image of their 'god' formed from Aaron's imagination. On that occasion, referring to the golden image fashioned by Aaron, the people said, "**These be thy gods, O Israel, which brought thee up out of the land of Egypt.**" (Exodus 32:4) They then proceeded to worship and offer sacrifices to that image.

Aaron's and the people's behaviors on that occasion were totally insulting to God! They basically claimed that a cow had rescued them from Egypt! Totally insulting!!! Baloney!!!

An image always represents someone or something. In the case of mankind, Adam, who was made in God's **image**, was supposed to represent God in the garden and on the earth.

Having made man in God's image, having placed him on earth, and having told Adam to take dominion over the earth and over all living creatures in it. Adam could accomplish all of those tasks because he was acting as God's representative. God could give new directions to Adam, and Adam could carry them out over all life on the planet because Adam was God's representative on earth. *Representation* corresponds to **image**.

The Likeness of God

Likeness, however, means "*resemblance*; concretely, *model, shape*." (Strong's) God created Adam in a form which resembled God. That is, Adam was created in God's **likeness**.

Now we do not know what God looks like. No one has ever seen Him. But all parts of Adam's body corresponded to the various parts and attributes of God. Adam could see, hear, taste, touch, smell, love, speak, reason, etc., because God had all of those abilities. Adam was created like God — that is, in God's **likeness**.

Free Will

An important characteristic of God's likeness which He placed in Adam is free will! All men, women, and children are clearly like God in this respect!

What beings can we describe which do **not** have free will? Puppets dangling from strings, and robots which perform according to well-defined programming, are two such groups — neither of which has free will.

Puppets behave according to the way their strings are manipulated. Robots are confined to behaving within the limits of their programming. No free will is possible from either of them.

As this book is being written, practically every current automobile manufacturer is designing, developing, and experimenting with self-drive automobiles. People step into them, tell the car where they want to go, and the car drives them there! It's like an automatic taxi — but no driver is involved. Do such cars have free will? No! Their programming may be extremely complex, but they can only function within the limited range of their programming.

High levels of sophistication and complexities of programming are **not** indicative of free will.

God created Adam with free will. He gave Adam the ability to freely choose how he would act, behave, think, etc. Along with free will comes the ability to enjoy fellowship with others — such as with God.

But Adam Sinned

Sin

When God tells us to do one thing and we choose to do the exact opposite, that is sin! . . . and that is the option we have with free will! I can choose to do as God asks! . . . or I can choose **not** to do as God asks! I have free will. It's my choice! . . . and choices like this are made all the time by every man, woman, and child!

As a little kid, I had the choice between obeying and **dis**obeying my parents! Usually, disobedience brought punishments! . . . but I had the choice! We have all had such experiences!

So why did God create man with free will if He knew that would open the door to sin? There are many possibilities for interesting conversations and fellowship among people who have free will. Everyone will not always agree with everyone else. My values, logic, experience, emotions, and moral compass lead me to think A! Your values, logic, experience, emotions, and moral compass applied to the exact same information may lead you to think B! We each are unique and we think, choose, feel, and reason differently.

When God says, "Dennis, do this!" and I have free will, I can say, "No, I won't!" and go my own way; or I can say, "Yes, I will!" That is free will! . . . and God knew this was possible when He created man.

When a person — any person — Adam, for example — chooses to disobey a direct order from God, that is sin! . . . and consequences will follow!

Adam and Eve

God created Adam and Eve with free will. He placed the two of them in Eden, the garden paradise He had prepared. God filled the garden of Eden with **every** fruit-bearing tree on the planet (and there are lots of them.) Then, God told Adam he could eat as much of whichever fruit he wanted — but not this one! . . . and He pointed at **one** tree!

One of the trees in the garden was the tree of life! When one eats regularly of the fruit of that tree, one can live forever! Notice: God placed **no** restrictions on eating the fruit of the tree of life! **None**! Adam and Eve could have eaten as much of its fruit as they wanted! They could have stuffed themselves on the fruit of the tree of life alone if they wanted! That would have been okay with God!

But God pointed at another tree — the tree of the knowledge of good and evil — and He told Adam he was not allowed to eat of the fruit of that **one** tree! **One** tree! . . . in a garden filled with trees of every type! **One**!

God's words were, "**Of every tree of the garden thou mayest freely eat: but of the tree of the knowledge of good and evil, thou shalt not eat of it: for <u>in the day that thou eatest thereof thou shalt surely die</u>.**" (Genesis 2:16-17) To disobey this command meant death!

There was no necessity for Adam nor Eve to eat fruit from that one tree. Let's make a conservative estimate: there are hundreds of different types and varieties of fruit on this planet. God basically told Adam, "Do not eat of this one tree! . . . but help yourselves to all of the rest! . . . and eat as much of them as you want!"

For all practical purposes, Adam's choice was infinite — actually, his choice was infinity minus one (for all you mathematicians out there: $\infty - 1$)! There was simply no need for Adam to eat of that one tree! He could have lived for eternity and never been bored with the selection of fruit available to him in the garden! He didn't **need** to ever touch that one tree's fruit!

God set this up to be a simple test! Adam had the choice: to obey or disobey! . . . and Adam failed the test!

Why Did God Make Us So We Can Sin?

Some people ask, "If God knew we **could** sin, why didn't He just make us so we **could not** sin?" The answer to this goes back to the earlier discussion about free will!

If I create a robot and program it to not touch a particular object, should I be surprised when it does not touch that object? If God did not give us freedom of choice in all matters, we would be a race of robots! If God wanted to fellowship with a race of people and have interesting discussions, interactions, and pleasant times with them, He had to create a race of people who were **like** Him, and He had to give them free will!

With Free Will, We Can Sin!

Why did God create mankind in the first place? As we have said, the answer appears to be that God wanted a people of His own (a family), whom He can love, and who will love Him in return!

Is such a relationship possible from a race of robots? No! . . . from a race of puppets? No! My son works in an automobile plant where the production line contains lots of workers, but some parts of the line are populated with robots. He may be able to walk over to the people who work on the line and fellowship with them. But can he fellowship with the robots on the line? No!

Sounds like a stupid question, doesn't it? If we were robots, or puppets, or if we were created in such a way that we **could not** sin — that is, if we were created **without** free will — would anyone **be able** to fellowship with us? Would anyone **want** to fellowship with us? I think not!

Robots in the movies are given human characteristics and abilities. But that's in the movies. We do not know how to do that in real life. Robots do not have favorites. They don't have favorite songs, or favorite movies, or favorite actors, or favorite friends, or favorite hobbies, etc.

God created us with free will, knowing full well that meant we could sin! . . . but free will gives us the opportunity to have favorites, to have likes, to have dislikes, to have independent opinions, etc.

Was God actually surprised when Adam sinned by eating some of the forbidden fruit? No. Disappointed? Yes. Surprised? No.

Why wasn't God surprised? Am I saying that God knew sin was coming from Adam? . . . and from Eve? . . . and from me? . . . and from you? Yes! He knew that would happen! Yes, He knew!

The Solution to the Sin Problem

If God knew, in advance, that mankind could sin, wouldn't that be a major problem for mankind? Yes, it would be! Yes, it is! What did God plan to do about sin, if anything? He planned to remedy the sin problem! Before the foundation of the world — that is, before God ever created anything — God knew He would need to deal with sin. He knew before the foundation of the world that He would need to provide a solution to the sin problem — because He knew mankind would not be able to solve the sin problem by themselves! . . . and with the cooperation of His Son, the Creator of the world, whom we know as Jesus Christ, God set His whole plan into motion!

Jesus volunteered, **"before the foundation of the world,"** to be the Redeemer of all mankind! (see 1 Peter 1:18-21) This whole plan was worked out in heaven before Genesis 1:1 ever took place!

What was God's reasoning? God gave man the freedom to choose, so all who freely choose to be His people, who want to love Him, to obey Him, and to spend time with Him, can (and will) spend eternity in fellowship with Him!

This also means that all those who choose **not** to have anything to do with God, don't **need** to have anything to do with Him!

God gave the children of Israel Ten Commandments, numerous other commandments, statutes, and directives, and over and over again, they refused to obey! They were dead set on doing their own thing! . . . and mostly, that is exactly what they did — their own thing! Along the way, they ignored and rejected God, only to choose instead to worship all manner of heathen idols, gods, and inanimate objects.

God said the solution to the sin problem was **not** for men to try to be good nor to do good deeds, because good behavior is impossible for natural man. God said the solution to the sin problem is to **believe**! . . . that is, to have **faith**!

God showed us Abraham, who set the example for all to follow!

Abraham believed God!   "**And he** [Abraham] <u>believed</u> **in the Lord; and He counted it to him for righteousness.**" (Genesis 15:6)

"**For what saith the scripture?   Abraham <u>believed</u> God, and it was counted unto him for righteousness.**" (Romans 4:3)

"**Even as Abraham <u>believed</u> God, and it was accounted to him for righteousness.**" (Galatians 3:6)

"**And the scripture was fulfilled which saith, 'Abraham <u>believed</u> God, and it was imputed unto him for righteousness: and he was called the Friend of God.' "** (James 2:23)

"**For God so loved the world, that He gave His only begotten Son, that whosoever <u>believeth</u> in Him should not perish, but have everlasting life.**" (John 3:16)

The fact that Abraham believed God is recorded often throughout the Bible.   Its frequency of appearance shows its importance!

For each of us, the solution to the sin problem is to put our faith in the Lord Jesus Christ.   **He** will handle that problem!   Actually, He **already** handled the sin problem!   How?   Jesus died and paid all penalties for **all** of **our** sins!   When we **believe** that **Jesus** paid all penalties for **our** sins as He suffered on the cross, He quickens us, and we are born again into the family of God!

Eternity Future

Who will spend eternity future in the presence of Jesus Christ and God the Father?   God's solution is really an elegant solution in this sense: **All** who **believe** Him will spend eternity with Him!   . . . and **only** those who **believe** Him will spend eternity with Him!

What about those who reject Him?   They will **not** be there!

God wanted to fellowship with mankind, to live with them, to be their God, to enjoy the love of all who want to be with Him!   Those are just exactly the people who will spend eternity in God's presence!

There is a saying: "You can choose your friends, but you cannot choose your family!"   Well in the case of God's family, that is false!   It does not apply!   God wants all of us in His family, but we can choose to join His family!   . . . or not!

All those who want to be with God, to love Him, to talk with Him, to fellowship with Him, and who are totally thankful for all He has done in their lives, can freely put their faith in Jesus Christ and spend eternity with Him!

All those who want nothing whatsoever to do with God, who do not believe He even exists, who do not believe He had anything to do with the creation of this world, who are not thankful to Him for anything, who do not want to spend any time with Him, and who do not want to fellowship with Him, will have nothing to do with Him throughout eternity! They will get their wish!

By giving mankind free will, and by handling the sin problem for mankind by Himself, God accomplished exactly what He wanted! He will be able to spend eternity fellowshipping with a precious people of His own! His people will love Him and rejoice to be with Him! . . . and He will love them and rejoice to be with them! It will make for a wonderful eternity!

It is a perfect solution!

"Thou Shalt Surely Die"!

Now, back to Adam. God told Adam that if he ate any of the fruit of the forbidden tree, **"Thou shalt surely die."** It is not clear that Adam even understood the concept of *death*. Had Adam ever seen or experienced death? We don't know.

Now, note the order of events in Genesis 2. God commanded Adam not to eat of **"the tree of the knowledge of good and evil,"** (vs 17) and after that, He formed Eve. So Eve was not present to hear God's actual words. Surely, Eve learned God's command about the forbidden fruit when Adam explained the rules of the garden to her.

The devil (the serpent), however, who understood the concepts of sin and death, declared to Eve that God's command to Adam was **not** true! The serpent called it a lie! He convinced Eve that God's declaration (**"Thou shalt surely die"**) concerned physical death — and the serpent assured Eve she would **not** surely die. According to the devil, one bite of the apple and instant death, ala Snow White, would **not** happen! **"And the serpent said unto the woman, 'Ye shall not surely die.' "** (Genesis 3:4)

As we know, Satan's words were the lie! . . . but Eve believed Satan. She did not trust Adam's explanation of the Lord's words.

Before they sinned, the spirits of both Adam and Eve were alive to God! They had been created and placed in the garden where they could have easy access to, and fellowship with, God! Everything was wonderful! . . . until Eve took a bite of the forbidden fruit, and then gave some to Adam to eat also.

In that instant, their spirits died to God! Close fellowship with God would be much more difficult (if not impossible)! No more wonderful, idyllic garden! Yes — they didn't instantly die physically. . . . but they did instantly die spiritually! . . . and the process was set in motion so they would eventually die physically. Why? . . . following their sin, and spiritual death to God, God no longer allowed them access to the tree of life. Without nourishment from the tree of life, they would eventually die physically. . . . and they did!

So Satan's words were proven to be the lie! God hadn't lied to Adam! Satan lied to Eve! Spiritual death to God was instantaneous! Physical death took a long time, but eventually, it happened.

God's words, **"Thou shalt surely die,"** were 100% accurate!

What Happened to Adam and Eve?

Both Adam and Eve sinned! They directly disobeyed a command of God! Eve was deceived by the serpent into disobeying. (1 Timothy 2:13) But Adam was not deceived. With his eyes wide open, Adam simply chose to disobey God! Adam chose to follow Eve's lead, and eat some of the forbidden fruit!

When God asked Adam what he had done, he pointed at Eve and said, **"She gave me of the tree, and I did eat."** (Genesis 3:12) That is, Adam pointed at Eve and said, "It's her fault!" Adam's second excuse even implied it was God's fault — because God had given the woman to him, and the woman gave him the fruit to eat. **"The woman whom Thou gavest to be with me, she gave me of the tree, and I did eat."** In reality, the whole choice was Adam's and he chose to disobey!

Adam wasn't the only one who tried to pass the buck. When God asked Eve what she had done, she answered, **"The serpent beguiled me, and I did eat."** (Genesis 3:13) That is, and with a point of the finger toward the serpent, she said, "It's his fault!"

God did not ask the serpent about its part in this sin. God knew what it had done! . . . and God simply cursed the serpent!

Eve's Punishment

God told Eve, "**I will greatly multiply thy sorrow and thy conception; in sorrow thou shalt bring forth children; and thy desire shall be to thy husband, and he shall rule over thee.**" (Genesis 3:16)

That is, God said it was going to be difficult for Eve (and all women after her) to carry and bear children! . . . and there was not going to be any way for her (or for any of her female descendants) to avoid it because her desire (and theirs) would be "**to thy husband.**"

We see the outworking of this in today's pregnancy rates. Women cannot stay away from men! . . . and those relationships lead to pregnancies! . . . some wanted, many not!

Adam's Punishment

Then, God turned to Adam and said, "[17] . . . **Because thou hast hearkened unto the voice of thy wife, and hast eaten of the tree, of which I commanded thee, saying, 'Thou shalt not eat of it:' cursed is the ground for thy sake; in sorrow shalt thou eat of it all the days of thy life;** [18]**thorns also and thistles shall it bring forth to thee; and thou shalt eat the herb of the field;** [19]**in the sweat of thy face shalt thou eat bread, till thou return unto the ground; for out of it was thou taken: for dust thou art, and unto dust shalt thou return.**" (Genesis 3:17-19)

God cursed the ground for Adam's sake. In simple English, the earth was going to bring forth weeds abundantly from that day forward! To farm the land, Adam, and all farmers after him, would need to deal with an abundance of weeds, thorns, and thistles to produce vegetables for their tables!

God also explained to Adam that eventually, he was going to die, be buried in the ground, and his body would revert back to the dust from which he was made. With Adam's sin came death! . . . physical death!

God did three more things that day! God sacrificed innocent animals to make coverings for the sin of Adam and Eve; He kicked Adam and Eve out of the garden; and He set up guards (cherubim) to prevent their return to the garden and their access to the tree of life!

"**Unto Adam also and to his wife did the LORD God make coats of skins, and clothed them.**" (Genesis 3:21) Some innocent animals gave their lives to provide the skins God used to clothe Adam and Eve! These were the first sacrifices in the Bible! Innocent animals were sacrificed to cover the nakedness — the result of the sins — of Adam and Eve!

By doing this, God showed Adam and Eve that there was a solution to their sins — the death of an innocent! . . . but it would be many years before God sent His Son to die for the sins of all mankind! A hint to that future solution, however, was shown here in Genesis 3.

Having kicked Adam and Eve out of the garden, God set **"cherubims, and a flaming sword which turned every way,"** (Genesis 3:24) to guard the entrance to Eden and **"to keep the way of the tree of life."**

Adam fell, Eve fell, the earth fell, and Satan (who had already fallen) was cursed — all because Adam took one bite of the forbidden fruit! All of this happened due to one act of disobedience — by Adam!

5

God's Image & Likeness Lost

The Earth Not in Subjection to Man

There was another major consequence of Adam's sin. Having fallen and been kicked out of the garden of Eden, Adam was no longer God's representative on earth. He had lost **the image** of God! Not only had he lost God's image, but Adam had also lost **the likeness** of God!

God had nothing to do with sin! So a sinful Adam was no longer representative of God on earth! We also know that "**God is a Spirit.**" (John 4:24) When Adam sinned, his spirit died to God immediately! This means he was no longer like God.

These were major consequences of Adam's sin! Fallen Adam no longer bore the image of God. He no longer represented God on earth. . . . and he was no longer like God either!

With reference to Adam's sin, the author of Hebrews explained the consequences of the fall of man:

"**⁶But one in a certain place testified, saying,**
'**What is man, that Thou art mindful of him?**
Or the son of man, that Thou visitest him?
⁷Thou madest him a little lower than the angels;
Thou crownedst him with glory and honour,
And didst set him over the works of Thy hands:
⁸Thou hast put all things in subjection under his feet.'

For in that He put all in subjection under him, He left nothing that is not put under him.

But now we see not yet all things put under him.

31

⁹**But we see Jesus, who was made a little lower than the angels for the suffering of death, crowned with glory and honour; that He by the grace of God should taste death for every man."** (Hebrews 2:6-9)

Verse 6 shows that there is a special relationship between God and man, as we have been explaining. ... and the Psalmist (vs 6, quoted from Psalm 8:4) inquired about that relationship!

Verses 7-8 show how man was created. He **"set him over the works of Thy hands,"** and all creation was placed **"in subjection under his feet."**

But the last third of verse 8 shows that did not happen: Adam did not take dominion over the earth! Everything on earth was not subject to Adam, nor to mankind after him! God's plans for man had not come to pass! ... and those plans would not come to fruition for many years! Verse 9, however, explains how God fixed this mess.

Jesus came to earth and **"was made a little lower than the angels,"** (vs 9) just like Adam had been made. (vs 7) Jesus was made a little lower than the angels **"for the suffering of death,"** unlike Adam. Jesus was **"crowned with glory and honour,"** just like Adam had been crowned. (vss 7 & 9) Jesus was crowned with glory and honour, **"that He by the grace of God should taste death for every man,"** unlike Adam.

Adam was created to take dominion over the works of God's hands (vs 7c), all was put in subjection under him (vs 8), and he failed in that task when he sinned! ... and according to the author of Hebrews, **"But now we see not yet all things put under him."** (vs 8c)

When Adam failed, he died! Spiritual death was immediate. Physical death came after a long life.

Jesus came to earth to set everything in order. He came **"for the suffering of death,"** and **"that He by the grace of God should taste death for every man."** (vs 9)

Adam was created to take dominion; he failed; and he died! Jesus came to earth to die; in doing so, He took dominion; He successfully set all things right; and He lives!

These verses in Hebrews 2 are powerful verses which compare and contrast **"the first man Adam"** with **"the last Adam,"** and **"the first man"** Adam with **"the second man,"** which is **"the Lord from heaven."** (1 Corinthians 15:45, 47)

Adam failed; Jesus succeeded!

Adam's Image

Notice in Genesis 5:3, that Adam passed his fallen image on to his son Seth. **"And Adam lived an hundred and thirty years, and begat a son in his own likeness, after his image; and called his name Seth."**

As a sinner, Adam no longer represented God on earth. As we will see in coming chapters, God Himself needed to come personally to live among the children of Israel to have a presence on earth. There was no one to represent God on earth, except for fallen men.

Eventually, God sent His Son, Jesus, to be born to Mary, to live as a man, and to represent God on earth to mankind.

Notice: Seth was born in **Adam's** image! . . . not God's image! . . . and Seth is representative of all children and descendants of Adam! Adam, who no longer carried the image of God, no longer represented God on earth! Seth, however, was fully representative of his father Adam! Everything that Adam had become on that day in the garden when he sinned and when God handed out punishments for that sin, was passed on to his children, such as Seth, and to all the rest of Adam's descendants!

Even unto today, and throughout all the intervening years, all of Adam's descendants have been fully representative of Adam in his sinful, fallen state. That is, all of Adam's descendants bear **the image of Adam**!

Adam's Likeness

Genesis 5:3 indicates that Seth was born **like** his father. The likeness of God had been lost by Adam the day he fell, but the likeness of Adam's fallen state passed fully on to his son Seth!

When Adam sinned, his spirit died to God. Without a spirit which was alive to God, Adam was on his own! Seth was born in that likeness! Seth not only inherited the sin nature from his father, but Seth's spirit was dead to God also. So Seth's tendency was to commit sins, just like his father's.

And since neither Adam, nor Eve, nor their children, nor their descendants had any access to the tree of life, they were all going to live their lives and die! As Paul wrote, **"For the wages of sin is death . . ."** (Romans 6:23)

They would all live difficult lives on earth, work hard all their days, and they would eventually die and revert back to the dust of the earth. Death is the main consequence of sin!

The Lord's Image Is Still Important

Even though we are no longer representative of God, nor are we any longer like Him, the fact that Adam was made in God's image is still important!

How? Anyone who sheds man's blood is to be put to death! Why? . . . because Adam was made in God's image!

Adam may no longer have been representative of God, and we are not representative of God either, but the fact that mankind was created in the image of God says that the blood of all mankind — which is the life of mankind — is still precious in God's sight!

Anyone who sheds man's blood is answerable to God! Because the life of man is in the blood, whoever sheds man's blood is guilty of murder — and shall be put to death! (Genesis 9:5-6)

This is an important point! The blood of man is the life of man! That has not changed since the day Adam was created. . . . and the unauthorized shedding of that blood by man has consequences!

A side note, but an important one in today's society, is that **all abortions, and most especially late-term abortions, are acts in which the blood of man is shed.** The pro-choice, pro-abortion crowd does not want to admit this, but abortions are murder! Why? . . . because the blood of babies (man) is shed by these heinous acts! . . . and that means abortions are covered by these admonitions and rules presented in Genesis 9!

Summary

When Adam sinned in the garden of Eden, he lost the **image** and **likeness** of God in which God had formed him. Adam passed his fallen image and fallen likeness to his son Seth and to all his descendants.

Seth was not representative of God, nor was he like God! . . . but Seth was fully representative of his father Adam, and fully like his fallen father! Seth was born in Adam's **image** and **likeness**!

Here we are today nearly 6000 years later, and we are still fully representative of, and like, fallen Adam! All mankind born on this earth, who are descendants of Adam and Eve, like Seth, have been born in Adam's image and likeness! We are all sinners! . . . thanks to Adam!

A New Beginning
With Noah

Adam may have sinned and fallen out of favor with God, but God did not give up on mankind. There were still a few descendants of Adam who wanted to worship God (Enoch, for example, Genesis 5:22) and with whom He was able to fellowship. Nevertheless, several generations later, the world of man had become so corrupt that God decided to start over!

Man's Deteriorated State

After the fall of Adam, everything went downhill! The Lord was not even close to being able to have fellowship with mankind. In fact, most of mankind wanted nothing to do with God!

Consider the state of mankind about 1500 years after the Creation in Noah's day:

"**And GOD saw that the wickedness of man was great in the earth, and that every imagination of the thoughts of his heart was only evil continually.**" (Genesis 6:5)

"**[11]The earth also was corrupt before God, and the earth was filled with violence. [12]And God looked upon the earth, and, behold, it was corrupt; for all flesh had corrupted His way upon the earth.**" (Genesis 6:11-12)

By this point in time, the state of the heart of man had declined so far that "**every imagination of the thoughts of his heart**" was evil —

37

"only evil continually"! God, who can hear the thoughts of man was bombarded with evil thoughts continually! That is difficult to fathom!

On top of that, the earth was "**corrupt**" and "**filled with violence.**" Anything to do with God and "**His way upon the earth,**" had also been corrupted.

Fortunately, we cannot hear the thoughts of the hearts of men, but God can! It must be terrible to see and hear your wonderful creation totally corrupted and destroyed to such an extent as it was in Noah's day!

All that was good in the earth was gone! Remember: after the sixth day of creation, we read, "**And God saw every thing that He had made, and, behold, it was very good . . .**" (Genesis 1:31) God stood back, took stock of His creation, and characterized it as "**very good.**"

By Noah's day, however, the world no longer resembled its original state! Mankind was totally corrupt! How could God fellowship with people like that? He could not!

One Bright Spot!

There was one bright spot in the whole evil world! Only one!

"**. . . Noah was a just man and perfect in his generations, and Noah walked with God.**" (Genesis 6:9)

In 1500 years, the earth's population surely numbered in the millions of people! Millions! . . . and there remained only one man who was "**just**" and "**perfect**" living on the earth. One! Noah! . . . and "**Noah walked with God.**" God could fellowship with Noah! . . . but he was the only one!

All the rest of mankind were evil! God would not have destroyed any just persons in the flood, so the fact that God destroyed all of mankind, except Noah and family, means that Noah was the only "**just**" person on earth at that time!

Since Noah walked with God, God would start mankind again from Noah and his wife (and their three sons and their wives)! . . . and He could continue His fellowship with Noah.

God's Decision

"⁶And it repented the LORD that He had made man on the earth, and it grieved Him at His heart. ⁷And the LORD said, 'I will destroy man whom I have created from the face of the earth; both man, and beast, and the creeping thing, and the fowls of the air; for it repenteth Me that I have made them." (Genesis 6:6-7)

It grieved the Lord's heart to see what mankind had done with His beautiful creation! Note that He didn't totally wipe mankind off the face of the earth. That surely was a possibility, but God didn't go that far. He came close! . . . but 8 saved is not **total** destruction.

God decided to start over! He would start with Noah and family, and two (male and female) of every kind of animal and fowl on earth! God was going to destroy every other living creature on earth — man and beast — and start again! He would start again with the one man who walked with Him: Noah!

To cleanse the earth, God decided to use a great flood! To save Noah and his family, God directed Noah to build an ark — a giant ship! In that ship, Noah, his family, and the animals, could safely endure the storm.

Notice again how many righteous people were in the ark: ONE! Moses wrote nothing about the characters of any other members of Noah's family. We know of only one just person on the ark: Noah.

We see a principle here which occurs throughout the Bible: the family of a righteous man (or woman) benefits from the relationship of that person to the Lord!

Noah was a just man! The Lord God saved Noah **and his family** through the flood due to Noah's relationship with God!

The Ark and the Flood

God told Noah to construct an "**ark**," because He was going to make it "**rain.**" In all likelihood, Noah had no idea what an *ark* was! . . . and because it did not rain on earth in those days, he probably did not know was *rain* was either!

The ark he was to build would be enormous! The Clemson University football stadium holds about 80,000 people. If the ark was placed in the football stadium, it would be about half as wide as the field, the bow would be in the stands behind the one end zone, and the stern would be in the stands behind the other end zone. The stadium is quite tall, and if the ark was sitting on the field, it would reach upwards to about half the height of the stadium. For its day, it was a gigantic ship!

Not only was the ark going to be enormous, but in 2500 B.C., Noah did not have modern cranes nor modern woodworking tools available to him! It was simply an enormous undertaking which God handed to Noah.

With that in mind, God gave Noah plenty of time to construct the ark! How long did it take to build? It only took Noah 100 years to build it! Imagine having locals asking what you were doing for 100 years! With this gigantic structure going up, Noah must have heard constantly, "What's that? What's an ark? What's rain?"

Not only did Noah have to build the ark, but he had to furnish it with enough food to last every creature in it for a whole year! It was a monumental task!

Surely God helped Noah round up the animals. After God told Noah it was time for everyone to enter the ark, when everyone was aboard, God sealed the ark's door from the outside!

The rains came as God said. They lasted 40 days and 40 nights. The flood waters remained for the better part of a year. Noah and company stayed in the ark for over a year, until it was safe to leave the ark and stand once again upon dry ground.

God's Command to Man and Beast

Having destroyed every living creature outside the ark, God told Noah and company when it was safe to leave the ark.

After everyone had departed the ark, God told Noah and family: **"Be fruitful, and multiply, and replenish the earth."** (Genesis 9:1)

Although God said this to Noah and family, this was also the task God set before all of the animals which endured the flood in the ark. They all needed to go out and replenish the earth with their kind, as well.

But after the flood, several distinct characteristics of the earth had changed.

No Longer Vegetarians

Before the flood, all living creatures, including man and beast, were vegetarians. After the flood, meat was added to the list of foods available to both man and beast.

"Every moving thing that liveth shall be meat for you; even as the green herb have I given you all things." (Genesis 9:3)

God forbade mankind, however, from eating the blood of any creature. Flesh was allowed for food; blood was not!

Rain Became Common

Before the flood, there was a mist which covered the earth and which kept it watered. After the flood, rain was common!

Rainbows

Also after the flood, rainbows were also common. The requirements for a rainbow are sunlight and rain.

God made a covenant with everyone in that day. He said that when **He** saw a rainbow, **He** would remember that **He** was never again going to flood the whole earth and wipe out all life.

It was a one-sided covenant. Noah and company needed to do nothing. They were but recipients of this covenant. God said from that day forward, every rainbow would remind Him of His covenant! . . . and He would never again flood the whole earth and destroy all life in it.

Summary

Due to extreme levels of evil and corruption on the earth, and by means of the great flood, God had wiped clean the whole earth and prepared it for a fresh start. The new start would come from Noah, his wife, his three sons, and their wives.

By means of the ark, eight people and a pair (male and female) of every created animal, were saved through the flood. All inhabitants of the ark represented the new, fresh start for the earth.

God was preparing once again to enjoy fellowship with mankind. Noah, after all, had walked with God before the flood. Having spent 100 years building the ark, there was no reason to believe Noah's relationship with God would change after the flood. Noah was a good starting point for the earth's repopulation.

7

But Noah's Reputation Was Tarnished

Noah Built An Altar

The very first thing Noah did after leaving the ark was to build an altar to the Lord! On that altar, he offered sacrifices unto God. Remember: there were two of every type of animal on the ark, male and female. But less well known — there were seven of each clean animal on the ark. This allowed Noah and family to make sacrifices and offerings of clean animals unto the Lord without extincting any of their species.

"And Noah builded an altar unto the LORD; and took of every clean beast, and of every clean fowl, and offered burnt offerings on the altar." (Genesis 8:20)

This was a great, and appropriate, first act of Noah and family after leaving the ark. It appears that Noah was continuing to walk justly before God.

In response to the burnt offerings, Moses wrote, **"And the LORD smelled a sweet savour; and the LORD said in His heart, 'I will not again curse the ground any more for man's sake; for the imagination of man's heart is evil from his youth; neither will I again smite any more every thing living, as I have done.' "** (Genesis 8:23)

That is, the Lord was pleased with Noah's worship! . . . and He promised never again to cleanse the whole earth of every living being!

Noah Planted A Vineyard

Almost the very next thing Noah did after leaving the ark, however, was to plant a vineyard, make wine, and get drunk!

"**[20]And Noah began to be an husbandman, and he planted a vineyard: [21]and he drank of the wine, and was drunken; and he was uncovered within his tent. [22]And Ham, the father of Canaan, saw the nakedness of his father, and told his two brethren without.**" (Genesis 9:20-22)

Getting drunk was a strike against Noah's just reputation — whether he knew wine could be intoxicating (which some have suggested he did not know), or not! Exposing himself, where his son could see him, was a bad result of being drunk. That didn't help his reputation either. One wonders: Where was his wife during this episode?

The son who saw his father uncovered was Ham. Judging by the words of verse 22 and following, Ham must have mocked Noah when he told his brothers what he had seen. His words to his brothers had to be insulting to his father. They most likely went something like this: "Hey, Shem! Japheth! You won't believe what I just saw! Ha! Ha! Ha!"

Noah's Reputation — Tarnished!

The two parts of this episode both tarnished Noah's reputation! So as much as we might like to think Noah remained just and perfect throughout his life, he demonstrated that he still had to deal with the enticements of the world, the flesh, and the devil as a descendant of fallen Adam.

After all, Noah and his sons were all born in the image and likeness of Adam! Evidence of the decline of mankind appears in the life of Noah after the flood!

God was still looking for members of His creation with whom He could fellowship. The downward slide, begun by Adam — even after man's fresh start brought about by the flood — appeared to be continuing with Noah and his sons, and it would continue with their descendants.

Nevertheless, it appears that Noah provided the Lord with quite a few years of good fellowship throughout his life! Surely, that was pleasing to the Lord!

The Chosen Family
of Abraham

The next man the Lord singled out was Abram, whose name the Lord later changed to Abraham.

The Lord Tells Abram to Depart

Abram and family were from Ur of the Chaldees which is on the Euphrates river southeast of Babylon. In today's world, Ur would be located in southeastern Iraq near its border with Kuwait.

Abram's father Terah had packed up his whole family and departed Ur for the land of Canaan, traveling first northwest to Haran. (Genesis 11:31) While in Haran, Terah died. Then, the Lord spoke to Abram.

The Lord told Abram that he should leave Haran and go to a land the Lord would show him. **"Now the LORD had said unto Abram, 'Get thee out of thy country, and from thy kindred, and from thy father's house, unto a land that I will shew thee."** (Genesis 12:1)

The rest of the Lord's statement to Abram on that occasion included several promises.

"²And I will make of thee a great nation, and I will bless thee, and make thy name great; and thou shalt be a blessing: ³and I will bless them that bless thee, and curse him that curseth thee: and in thee shall all families of the earth be blessed." (Genesis 12:2-3)

The Lord promised to make of Abram **"a great nation."** Here, we can see that the Lord had a people of His own in mind. The Lord was planning to make the family of Abram His family. He was going to care for them, bless them mightily, and give them the land of Canaan!

In addition, the Lord promised **to bless all families of the earth** through Abram's family! We find out from Paul's writings in the New Testament, that this promise in Genesis 12:3, is a statement of the Gospel of Jesus Christ!

"And the scripture, foreseeing that God would justify the heathen through faith, preached before the gospel unto Abraham, saying, 'In thee shall all nations be blessed.' " (Galatians 3:8)

These promises contained more long-range implications than Abram may have realized when he first heard them! It is not clear that many from the Old Testament, nor even many from the New Testament, would have recognized this promise as a statement of the Gospel had Paul not identified it as such!

But there it is! The Gospel, which is the Good News of the Lord Jesus Christ, was stated in Genesis 12:3! The Lord was going to bless all the nations of the world through Abram's family. . . . and specifically (we know this from hindsight), He was going to do this through Abram's descendant Jesus Christ!

Note also that these promises, including this statement of the Gospel, were made to Abram almost 2000 years before the Son of God, Jesus Christ, would even come to earth to live as a man!

Abram's descendants would become the nation of Israel — that is, the Jewish people! . . . and the whole world was going to be blessed by a descendant of Abram! The Lord made this promise to Abram all the way back in Genesis 12 — around 2000 BC. That's amazing!

Many people consider the Good News of the Gospel to be a New Testament concept! . . . and it is! The idea that it appears early in Genesis of the Old Testament, however, is a surprise to many!

With all of these promises in mind, Abram obeyed. Abram and family departed Haran to march southwest to Canaan. No further details of the Lord's command to Abram were immediately forthcoming. . . . but Abram obeyed!

The Land of Canaan

The Lord led Abram and company to the land of Canaan.

"And the LORD appeared unto Abram, and said, 'Unto thy seed will I give this land:' and there builded he an altar unto the LORD, who appeared unto him." (Genesis 12:7)

When the Lord spoke this to Abram, he and his company were near Sichem in the land of Canaan. Upon their arrival, Abram built an altar unto the Lord.

Next, Abram and company moved a little further east, where they again pitched their tents, and built another altar unto the Lord. The name of this place, originally known as the city Luz, was renamed at a later date to be known as **"Bethel"** which means "The house of God." (Newberry Bible, margin, Genesis 12:8)

"And he removed from thence unto a mountain on the east of Bethel, and pitched his tent, having Bethel on the west, and Hai on the east: and there he builded an altar unto the LORD, and called upon the name of the LORD." (Genesis 12:8)

Because there was a famine in the land, Abram and company packed up and continued traveling. Note that Abram did not check with the Lord before deciding to go to Egypt. If he did check first, Moses didn't mention it. Abram led the family south and west into the land of Egypt. There, they dwelt until the end of the famine. . . . and the Lord was with them in Egypt, watching over them.

Clearly, Abram was ready and willing to be obedient to the Lord's direction. When the famine ended, Abram and company departed Egypt and returned to Bethel/Hai, where he had set up his tent earlier. Once again, **"Abram called on the name of the LORD."** (Genesis 13:4)

It was beginning to look like the Lord God had found a man who appreciated Him, and with whom He could fellowship.

Upon their return from Egypt, both Abram and Lot had an abundance of flocks, herds, tents, and possessions. The land was not large enough for both families and their possessions. So they split up. Lot went east, across the river Jordan, and then south, settling east of the Dead sea. Abram remained in Canaan.

The Lord's Promise to Abram

After Lot departed with his family and possessions, the Lord reaffirmed His promises to Abram.

"**¹⁴And the LORD said unto Abram, after that Lot was separated from him, 'Lift up now thine eyes, and look from the place where thou art northward, and southward, and eastward, and westward: ¹⁵for all the land which thou seest, to thee will I give it, and to thy seed for ever. ¹⁶And I will make thy seed as the dust of the earth: so that if a man can number the dust of the earth, then shall thy seed also be numbered.'** " (Genesis 13:14-16)

For his obedience, the Lord promised Abram all of the land which he could see around him! He promised this land to Abram and to his innumerable descendants "**for ever**"!

The Lord didn't demand any more of Abram! Abram moved his tent once again to Hebron, where he built another altar unto the Lord. Every place in which Abram pitched his tent, he built an altar unto the Lord.

This was the type of behavior the Lord was wanting to see out of the race of men. Abram obeyed the Lord's directions, and worshipped Him wherever he set up camp!

The Lord was a step closer to having a people of His own!

King Melchizedek

When four kings, led by Chedorlaomer attacked the lands and the cities in which Lot had taken up residence, they conquered the lands and carted off all the people as slaves. Among those slaves were Lot and all members of his house.

When Abram learned of this, he took all of his warriors, chased after Chedorlaomer, smote them, recovered all of the captives (including Lot and company), and took the spoil. Abram, however, kept none of the spoil for himself.

On their return from the battle, they encountered Melchizedek, king of Righteousness and king of Salem. As a priest of the Most High God, Melchizedek "**brought forth bread and wine.**" (Genesis 14:18)

"^{19}And he blessed him, and said, 'Blessed be Abram of the most high God, possessor of heaven and earth: ^{20}and blessed be the most high God, which hath delivered thine enemies into thy hand. And he gave him tithes of all." (Genesis 14:19-20)

When Melchizedek met with Abram, he not only blessed Abram, but he also blessed "**the most high God.**" During this meeting, Abram gave Melchizedek "**tithes of all.**" Melchizedek functioned as a priest between the Most High God and man. The order of Melchizedek was the order of which Jesus was Great High Priest! A more complete explanation of the relationship between Melchizedek and Jesus Christ can be found in Hebrews 7.

Melchizedek was an Old Testament picture of Jesus Christ. In the New Testament, Jesus Christ is called "**great high priest.**" (Hebrews 4:14) Jesus was not great high priest of the Levitical order "**after the order of Aaron,**" but of "**the order of Melchisedec.**" (Hebrews 7:11) It is important to note that the order of Melchizedek predates the Levitical order and it continues today and forever!

Notice that Melchizedek brought forth bread and wine, which points forward to the times of remembrance requested by Jesus Christ in the New Testament. Bread and wine are at the center of the remembrance feast, instituted by Jesus Christ, who is a priest forever of the order of Melchizedek! There are many interesting parallels between Melchizedek in Genesis 14, and Jesus Christ in the New Testament.

For Abram's part, he freely blessed the Most High God because he knew that it was only through the Lord's help that he and his men were able to rescue Lot and family from king Chedorlaomer. Then, Abram paid tribute to the Lord by giving tithes to Melchizedek!

An Exceeding Great Reward

Upon returning to the land of Canaan, we read of a new promise the Lord made to Abram:

"**After these things the word of the LORD came unto Abram in a vision, saying, 'Fear not, Abram: I am thy shield, and thy exceeding great reward.'** " (Genesis 15:1)

Abram asked what that reward might be? The Lord promised Abram an heir with his wife Sarai. (Genesis 15:4) The Lord's first promise said that Abram's descendants of this heir would be as numerous as the dust of the earth. (Genesis 13:16) This time, the Lord told Abram to look to the stars in the sky: his descendants would be as numerous as they!

"And He brought him forth abroad, and said, 'Look now toward heaven, and tell the stars, if thou be able to number them:' and He said unto him, 'So shall thy seed be.' " (Genesis 15:5)

At this point, Abram had two promises from the Lord. (1) The Lord promised Abram an earthly people, as numerous as the sand by the sea; and (2) the Lord promised Abram a heavenly people, as numerous as the stars in the sky!

Many consider such promises totally preposterous! Nevertheless, the Lord made these two promises to Abram! Hindsight tells us that the children of Israel were this innumerable earthly people. We also learn from Paul that all believers in Jesus Christ comprise the heavenly people! Consider Paul's words:

"24Wherefore the law was our schoolmaster to bring us unto Christ, that we might be justified by faith. 25But after that faith is come, we are no longer under a schoolmaster.

26For ye are all the children of God by faith in Christ Jesus.

27For as many of you as have been baptized into Christ have put on Christ. 28There is neither Jew nor Greek, there is neither bond nor free, there is neither male nor female: for ye are all one in Christ Jesus.

29And if ye be Christ's, then are ye Abraham's seed, and heirs according to the promise." (Galatians 3:24-29)

The last verse in this passage teaches that all believers in Christ are members of **"Abraham's seed."** This is the heavenly people the Lord promised Abraham.

Throughout Old Testament times and on into Jesus' day, the Jewish people were the earthly people the Lord promised Abraham. But they rejected the Lord during Old Testament times, and they rejected and crucified the Son of God, Jesus Christ, when He came to live among them. They were descendants of Abraham in the flesh, but not believers in Jesus Christ. . . . not yet anyway!

One day coming, that will change and the whole nation of Israel (all who are living at the time) will recognize that Jesus Christ truly is their Messiah! When that day comes, they will all put their faith in Him! They will believe as a whole people! . . . and as a whole nation they will join God's heavenly people! That day is near, but yet future!

Abram Believed God!

There is some background to these two promises which we did not mention. Abram's wife, Sarai, was barren. They had no son! . . . and yet the Lord was promising them innumerable descendants! Actually, the Lord promised the two of them that they, together, would have a son — even in their old age!

What was Abram's response? **"And he believed in the LORD; and He counted it to him for righteousness."** (Genesis 15:6)

Abram believed God! . . . and the Lord counted it as righteousness in Abram! That is, the Lord God credited righteousness to Abram's account!

Note: Abram still had done very little directly toward God, but he believed God! . . . and God credited him with righteousness for that belief!

The Lord Appeared to Abram

When Abram was 99 years old, the Lord appeared to him again. First, the Lord identified Himself to Abram: **"I am the Almighty God; walk before Me, and be thou perfect."**

Then the Lord confirmed the covenant He had made with Abram: **"And I will make My covenant between Me and thee, and will multiply thee exceedingly."** (Genesis 17:2) As God spoke to him, Abram fell down on his face before Him!

The Lord God said, **"⁴As for Me, behold, My covenant is with thee, and thou shalt be a father of many nations. ⁵Neither shall thy name any more be called Abram, but thy name shall be Abraham; for a father of many nations have I made thee. ⁶And I will make thee exceeding fruitful, and I will make nations of thee, and kings shall come out of thee. ⁷And I will establish My covenant between Me and thee and thy seed after thee in their generations for an everlasting covenant, to be a God unto thee, and to thy seed after thee. ⁸And I will give unto thee, and to thy seed after thee, the land wherein thou art a stranger, all the**

land of Canaan, for an everlasting possession; and I will be their God."
(Genesis 17:4-8)

On this occasion, God gave Abram a new name: *Abraham*. The
name *Abram* means "Exalted father." *Abraham* means "Father of a
multitude." (Newberry Bible, margin, Genesis 17:5) The new name is
consistent with, and reflects, the Lord's promise to him.

God said, "**I will establish My covenant . . . to be a God unto
thee, and to thy seed after thee.**" With this promise — an everlasting
promise — God had identified a people of His Own!

In case Abraham wasn't listening carefully, the Lord repeated: He
was giving the land of Canaan to Abraham and to his "**seed after thee,**" as
"**an everlasting possession,**" AND God said, "**I will be their God.**"

We note again: the Lord God had identified His chosen people!
The Lord's people on earth would be the seed of Abraham!   . . . and in
return, He said, "**I will be their God.**"

There were only two problems as Abraham and Sarah saw it: (1)
Abraham was 99, and (2) Sarah was 90. Both thought they were past child-
bearing age!

The Sign of the New Covenant

To confirm that Abraham and family had a covenant with the
Lord, all men of Abraham's family were to be circumcised! Abraham and
all the men of his family complied!

Note: no one but the person circumcised, and God, would know
of this sign! This was a private sign between each man in Abraham's
family and God! The important part of this sign was that **God knew** of it!

A Son Would Be Born to Abraham and Sarah

Once again, God promised Abraham and Sarah a son! "**And I
will bless her, and give thee a son also of her: yea, I will bless her, and she
shall be a mother of nations; kings of people shall be of her.**" (Genesis
17:16)

Abraham's response to this was to fall on the floor laughing!
(Genesis 17:17) At a later time, Sarah heard the Lord make this same
promise, and she laughed, too! (Genesis 18:12)

This is significant because laughing at the Lord's promise is indicative that Abraham and Sarah were really questioning God's ability to fulfill this promise. But they believe Him, and a year later, they did have the son He promised!

A Son Is Born to Abraham and Sarah

Sure enough, when Abraham was 100 years old and Sarah was 91, Sarah gave birth to a son!

What was the boy's name? God told them to call him "**Isaac**" which means "He shall laugh." (Newberry Bible, margin, Genesis 21:3)

The Lord promised them a son, and in their old age, Sarah gave birth to a son! . . . and due to the name the Lord chose for the boy, we know that **He was fully aware** they both laughed at His promise to give them a son!

The Lord Tests Abraham

Years later, the Lord tested Abraham. He told Abraham to take Isaac up onto the mountain and offer him as a burnt sacrifice to the Lord.

"And He said, 'Take now thy son, thine only son, Isaac, whom thou lovest, and get thee into the land of Moriah, and offer him there for a burnt offering upon one of the mountains which I will tell thee of.' " (Genesis 22:2)

Without any argument, Abraham got up early the next morning and prepared to go do as the Lord had directed. Abraham took Isaac, and two of his servants, and they rode up onto the mountain to offer sacrifice.

When they arrived at the spot up on the mountain, we read:

"And Abraham said unto his young men, 'Abide ye here with the ass; and I and the lad will go yonder and worship, and come again to you.'" (Genesis 22:5)

This was a major test of Abraham's faith in God! But notice: Abraham told the young men to wait there while he and Isaac went up the mountain to worship. Abraham finished that sentence by adding that they would **"come again to you."** Abraham believed both he and Isaac would return to his men — together.

Abraham didn't know what was going to happen, or how it was going to happen, but he trusted the Lord. Isaac was the child of promise, so the Lord had great plans for him! How could Isaac be the father of an innumerable people if he was dead?

The writer of Hebrews explained that Abraham was "**accounting that God was able to raise him up, even from the dead; from whence also he received him in a figure.**" (Hebrews 11:19)

Abraham didn't know God's plans for Isaac up on the mountain, but the Lord had promised to do great things with Isaac's descendants! So Abraham thought, as explained in Hebrews, that if the Lord actually made Abraham carry out the sacrifice, the Lord would raise Isaac up from the dead! . . . and in faith, Abraham fully intended to offer Isaac as a burnt offering to the Lord as commanded!

Isaac even asked Abraham, "**where is the lamb for a burnt offering?**" (Genesis 22:7) They carried with them everything they needed to make a sacrifice unto the Lord — everything but a lamb for the sacrifice! . . . and Isaac noticed!

Abraham knew that Isaac was the sacrifice the Lord directed him to make. Isaac didn't learn until they were in the final stages of preparation up on the mountain.

So they went up the mountain, stacked the wood for the fire, and then Abraham bound Isaac and placed him on the wood. When he was about to strike Isaac with the knife, the Lord stopped him!

An angel of the Lord called out to Abraham at that very instant and said, "**Lay not thine hand upon the lad, neither do thou any thing unto him: for now I know that thou fearest God, seeing thou hast not withheld thy son, thine only son from Me.**" (Genesis 22:12)

When Abraham looked up, he saw "**a ram caught in a thicket by his horns.**" (Genesis 22:13) Abraham then released Isaac and offered the ram as a burnt offering unto the Lord.

The Lord had His answer! Abraham had great faith in Him! Abraham believed God!

God's Family on Earth

Here, God clearly identified His chosen family on earth: it would include all descendants of Abraham through his son Isaac! They would be God's people, and He would be their God!

This is what the Lord wanted! . . . but these people were still sons and daughters of Adam — born in Adam's image and likeness! The sin problem would continue to rear its ugly head — again and again and again!

The question was: Would Abraham's descendants accept the Lord God as their leader and their God? That remained to be seen!

Abraham Acted
Independently of the Lord

Needless to say, Abraham was a great man among men! Among the Jews, Abraham is revered as the first of the Patriarchs. But that does not mean he was perfect — or without flaws. Abraham enjoyed great fellowship with the Lord over many years, which is exactly what the Lord wanted from mankind!

But Abraham was a sinner just like the rest of us. He showed this early in his relationship with the Lord. He trusted the Lord's promises — but he did not trust Him completely. . . . and when he did not trust the Lord, their fellowship suffered! Maybe his sins were small, but a sin is a sin! . . . and Abraham sinned!

Remember: Abraham was born in the image and likeness of **Adam,** just like the rest of us, so he, too, had to deal with indwelling sin!

Abraham trusted the Lord! He believed the Lord! . . . and that belief was credited to his account!

God was fully aware, however, that Abraham was a sinner! . . . that Abraham was fully human. . . . but He also knew that Abraham believed Him! So He chose Abraham and his descendants to be His people on earth.

Abraham Didn't Always Trust the Lord

What evidence is there that Abraham didn't completely trust the Lord? We will look at some indications of this in Abraham's life.

Where to Set Up Camp?

The Lord told Abraham to leave his home to go to the land of Canaan. He did! . . . but when Abraham arrived in Canaan, did he ask the Lord where in Canaan He wanted him to make his residence? No.

He stopped in Sichem, set up camp, and built an altar. According to Moses' account, Abraham made that decision himself. Then, he moved east of Bethel, set up camp, and built another altar. That appeared good!

Abraham traveled all that way from Ur to Haran to Canaan at the Lord's direction, and then he appears to have made the last few decisions on his own. For someone under the guidance of the Lord, it seems he should have asked for a specific location in which to set up camp. Moses did not record any such questions.

Where to Endure the Famine?

When a famine hit, Abraham didn't inquire of the Lord whether to stay or leave. He gathered up his family and departed to Egypt. (Genesis 12:9) This appears to be another unilateral decision Abraham made — without any consultation with the Lord.

The Lord had just brought him a long distance from Ur to the land of Canaan, which the Lord promised to give to Abraham. But when the famine hit, Abraham packed up and left for another country.

Had he asked, the Lord might have told him to stay in Bethel, where the Lord would take care of him. There is no record that Abraham asked, nor any record that the Lord volunteered such directions.

So Abraham and family traveled to Egypt.

What to Do with A Beautiful Wife?

The previous two points about asking the Lord where to live and whether or not to stay, are minor. If Abraham completely trusted the Lord, one would expect he should have checked for the Lord's counsel on those two decisions. . . . but he didn't.

Abraham's decision to lie about his relationship to his wife, however, is a much bigger deal. It shows that Abraham was not fully reliant on the Lord!

With respect to Abraham and Sarah's safety, Abraham should have trusted the Lord. He should have consulted the Lord about it. . . . but again, he did not. Abraham made this decision out of fear for his life. He wasn't worried about Sarah's life — he was worried about his own life! Maybe, they shouldn't have been in Egypt in the first place! Had they stayed in Canaan, there would have been no need for him to fear for his life, nor to conspire with his wife to tell this lie.

Abraham foresaw a problem in Egypt: Sarah was a *beautiful* woman. Abraham described her as "**fair**." (Genesis 12:11) He feared that the Egyptians would see that she was a beautiful woman, kill her husband (him), and take her for their own. Apparently, that was a common practice by the powerful in their day!

One would think Abraham might have been concerned about the safety of his wife — but he was more concerned about his own safety.

What was their solution? Abraham and Sarah agreed; they would claim she was his sister. (Genesis 12:13) This was a **half-truth**: Abraham and Sarah were born to the same father, Terah, of different mothers. So they were half-brother and half-sister. They decided they simply would not tell the truth to anyone — that Sarah was actually Abraham's **wife**.

This shows that neither Abraham nor Sarah were relying on the Lord to keep them safe. When the Lord told them to do something, they obeyed. . . . but they didn't consult Him when they foresaw problems. The fact that the Lord had made wonderful promises to Abraham regarding the land of Canaan, suggests Abraham should have trusted the Lord to protect him.

The Egyptians took one look at Sarah and concluded that she was "**very fair**" — that is, *very beautiful!* (Genesis 12:14) Since she said she wasn't married, the princes took her into Pharaoh's house. (Genesis 12:15)

At that point, the Lord intervened! He put plagues on Pharaoh and his house because they took Sarah away from Abraham. (Genesis 12:17)

When Pharaoh learned that Abraham and Sarah were husband and wife, Pharaoh wanted to know why Abraham had lied to him. (Genesis 12:18-19) Abraham explained, and Pharaoh commanded his men to send Abraham and Sarah away! (Genesis 12:20)

Notice that even though Abraham **never** asked the Lord about their plan to lie about their true relationship, the Lord was watching out for them, and He intervened when necessary! He protected both Abraham and Sarah while they were among the Egyptians!

Same Problem On A Later Occasion

The Lord's big covenant which He made with Abraham appears in Genesis 17. There, he changed Abram's name to Abraham, and Sarai's name to Sarah. The Lord was going to do great things with Abraham and Sarah and with their seed.

One might think that having renewed such a covenant with the Lord, Abraham and Sarah would be more reliant on Him! One might also think that having been kept safe by the Lord during their stay in Egypt, that also might have made them more reliant on Him! Right??

Wrong! In Genesis 20, Abraham and Sarah traveled to the Philistine city of Gerar and dwelt there for a time. Once again, they agreed that Sarah should claim she was Abraham's sister! (Genesis 20:2)

Consider these circumstances: Abraham was 99; Sarah was 90; and Abraham had just fallen on the floor laughing when the Lord told him Sarah was going to bear him a son. In Abraham's eyes, they were clearly too old to have a child! . . . but when they traveled to Gerar, they agreed again to tell everyone Sarah was his sister. Abraham again feared for his life because of his beautiful wife!

Moses did not record that Abraham asked counsel of the Lord to learn if they should even be in Gerar. Neither did Abraham request protection of the Lord. He and Sarah simply decided to reside for a while in the Philistine region (Gerar) and to again claim she was his sister.

This time, the incident involved Abimelech, king of Gerar. When Abraham declared to him that Sarah was his sister, Abimelech immediately took her into his house.

God intervened again on behalf of Abraham and Sarah. God spoke to Abimelech in a dream. He told Abimelech that he was **"a dead man,"** because he had taken a woman who was **"a man's wife."** Abimelech defended himself, saying that Abraham told him Sarah was his sister! (Genesis 20:3)

Nevertheless, God had already inflicted Abimelech and his people with some type of plague that prevented them from having children. **"For** the LORD had fast closed up all the wombs of the house of Abimelech, because of Sarah Abraham's wife." (Genesis 20:18)

Abimelech then restored Sarah to Abraham, and told them they could dwell wherever they wanted in the land of Gerar. Abraham prayed to the Lord on Abimelech's behalf, and He removed the plague He had placed on Abimelech and his people.

Abimelech asked Abraham why he had lied to him! "What hast thou done unto us?" (Genesis 20:9) Abraham answered, "Because I thought, Surely the fear of God is not in this place; and they will slay me for my wife's sake." (Genesis 20:11)

This statement shows that Abraham did not consult the Lord before moving to Gerar nor before making the pact with his wife. Abraham did not trust the people of Gerar; he made assumptions based on zero information; and he again feared for his life (not Sarah's). All of this he did without consulting the Lord!

Abraham made these decisions on his own. In those days, some of his actions were inspired and empowered by God, but some of his actions were nevertheless decided independently!

Abraham And Sarah Thought God Needed Their Help

The Lord promised Abraham an heir with his wife Sarah. (Genesis 15:4) When he heard this, Abraham fell on the floor laughing! (Genesis 17:17)

Nevertheless, the Lord spoke repeatedly of Abraham's promised seed. (Genesis 15:18) Some of these references were to Abraham's numerous descendants — his "seed," plural. Some of these references were to Abraham's "seed," singular, the Son of God, Jesus Christ, who would be a descendant of Abraham. At the time, Abraham did not fully understand these distinctions.

In New Testament times, Paul understood, and provided the explanation. Paul wrote, "Now to Abraham and his seed were the promises made. He saith not, 'And to seeds,' as of many; but as of one, 'And to thy seed,' which is Christ." (Galatians 3:16, with reference to the Lord's words in Genesis 17:7)

Because Sarah believed that the LORD had restrained her from having a child, Sarah suggested that Abraham could have a son by fathering a child with Hagar, her handmaid. (Genesis 16:2) Abraham took his wife's advice! **"And Abraham hearkened to the voice of Sarah."** (Genesis 16:2)

So much for trusting and asking guidance of the Lord!

Abraham and Sarah Laughed

Regardless what the Lord told them, both Abraham and Sarah were skeptical about having a son together. They both considered themselves too old for that! They both considered the thought laughable! They gave the distinct impression that they weren't convinced the Lord's promise was even possible! . . . and they appeared to believe that the Lord needed help if Abraham was going to have an heir!

Yet, the Lord repeated His promise to Abraham and Sarah. **"And I will bless her, and give thee a son also of her: yea, I will bless her, and she shall be a mother of nations; kings of people shall be of her."** (Genesis 17:16) **"And God said, 'Sarah thy wife shall bear thee a son indeed . . .' "** (Genesis 17:19)

When Abraham heard, he laughed! (Genesis 17:17) The Lord's statement was so funny, Abraham fell down on the floor laughing!

Then, God repeated the promise of a son within hearing range of Sarah. . . . and Sarah laughed, too! (Genesis 18:12) When accused of laughing, however, she denied it! (Genesis 18:15) She lied! She did laugh!

The Lord told them that this son of promise (Genesis 17:21) would be called **"Isaac"** (Genesis 17:19), which means "Laughter." (Newberry Bible, margin, Genesis 17:19) It is clear from this the Lord knew their reactions to His promise because **He** chose the name *Isaac.*

The birth of Isaac occurred to Abraham when he was 100 years old and Sarah was 91. (Genesis 21:2) God didn't need their help to fulfill His promise! . . . and He fulfilled His promise even though they thought the impossible was hilarious!

Abraham Was A Descendant of Adam

The examples given above show that Abraham was a descendant of Adam. He was born in Adam's image and likeness!

None of these sins were particularly terrible. Abraham and Sarah didn't trust the Lord completely and didn't consult Him about many of their life's details. In those cases, they made decisions independently of the Lord's input. Nevertheless, the Lord chose Abraham to be the father of His earthly and heavenly people! . . . and Abraham's descendants would be known as the children of the Lord!

So in the Lord's desire to have a people of His own, He chose Abraham who was a believing and obedient servant. When the Lord told Abraham to do something, he obeyed. Abraham did act independently on several occasions, but when the Lord made wonderful promises to Abraham, he believed! . . . and the Lord made very great and wonderful promises indeed to Abraham and to his seed!

Throughout the history books, Abraham is portrayed as a great man — and he was! . . . but as a descendant of Adam, he still had to deal with indwelling sin. He was born, after all, in Adam's image and likeness — just like all the rest of us!

From God's point-of-view, He enjoyed fellowship with Abraham throughout his life. . . . and He was looking forward to more fellowship with Abraham's descendants. All the while, God knew that Abraham and all his descendants were dealing with indwelling sin!

The Line Continues to Isaac

10

The Lord promised Abraham that He would establish His covenant with his son Isaac and with Isaac's seed:

"And God said, 'Sarah thy wife shall bear thee a son indeed; and thou shalt call his name Isaac: and I will establish My covenant with him for an everlasting covenant, and with his seed after him." (Genesis 17:19)

"But My covenant will I establish with Isaac, which Sarah shall bear unto thee at this set time in the next year." (Genesis 17:21)

Isaac Cooperated When Abraham Was Tested

When the Lord sent Abraham up onto the mountain to offer his son Isaac as a burnt offering, Isaac complied with all of his father Abraham's requests. (Genesis 22)

We don't know how old Isaac was at the time, but we think he might have been a teenager — big enough to put up a struggle and not cooperate with Abraham. . . . but we read no such thing.

Isaac questioned what his father was about to do, but Moses did not record any struggle nor resistance from him.

Abraham Left All to Isaac

When Abraham was old and approaching death, he left all of his inheritance to Isaac:

"And Abraham gave all that he had unto Isaac." (Genesis 25:5)

The Lord Blesses Isaac

Following Abraham's death, the Lord turned to Isaac:

"**And it came to pass after the death of Abraham, that God blessed his son Isaac; and Isaac dwelt by the well Lahairoi.**" (Genesis 25:11)

Isaac was 40 when he married Rebekah. "**And Isaac intreated the LORD for his wife, because she was barren: and the LORD was intreated of him, and Rebekah his wife conceived.**" (Genesis 25:21)

When Isaac wanted a child, he took his plea to the Lord! . . . and Rebekah conceived and bore twins: Esau, the firstborn, and Jacob.

The Lord Promises Isaac

There was a famine in the land and Isaac sought help from Abimelech, king of the Philistines. Note that Isaac's first choice for help was not the Lord — it was the Philistine king! (Genesis 26:1) Isaac also intended to travel to Egypt to endure the famine. (vs 2)

This time, however, the Lord stepped in and told Isaac to stay and dwell in the land. If he stayed, God promised to be with him and bless him.

"[3]**Sojourn in this land, and I will be with thee, and will bless thee; for unto thee, and unto thy seed, I will give all these countries, and I will perform the oath which I sware unto Abraham thy father;** [4]**and I will make thy seed to multiply as the stars of heaven, and will give unto thy seed all these countries; and in thy seed shall all the nations of the earth be blessed;** [5]<u>**because that Abraham obeyed My voice**</u>**, and kept My charge, My commandments, My statutes, and My laws.**" (Genesis 26:3-5)

These are the same promises that the Lord made to Isaac's father Abraham. These promises also included another statement of the Gospel (vs 4), which Paul explained in the New Testament. (Galatians 3:16)

What was the difference between the promises to Abraham and the promises to Isaac? The Lord made the promises to Abraham because **Abraham** believed the Lord and obeyed His commandments. The Lord made all of these same promises to Isaac because **Abraham** obeyed the

Lord's voice (vs 5) and kept the Lord's charge, commandments, statutes, and laws!

The Lord didn't give these promises to Isaac because Isaac obeyed, nor because Isaac believed. He gave these promises to Isaac because **Abraham obeyed and Abraham believed!** Isaac was receiving the Lord's blessings because of his father's faith and obedience!

Note that when the famine hit in Abraham's day, Abraham packed up and went to Egypt. The Lord said nothing, but He protected Abraham and Sarah throughout that famine during their sojourn in Egypt.

When the famine hit in Isaac's day, Isaac also intended to pack up and go to Egypt. . . . but this time, the Lord stepped in and told him not to travel to Egypt but remain in the land. . . . and Isaac was obedient to that command. (Genesis 26:6)

The Lord Blesses Him Again

The Lord spoke to Isaac again, blessed him, and promised to multiply his seed **"for my servant Abraham's sake."** Although the Lord was with Isaac, we see He was intent on carrying out His promises **to Abraham** through his son Isaac!

"And the LORD appeared unto him the same night, and said, 'I am the God of Abraham thy father: fear not, for I am with thee, and will bless thee, and multiply thy seed for my servant Abraham's sake.' " Genesis 26:24)

Summary

Because Abraham believed God, the Lord promised to bless him and multiply his seed forever! Abraham's son of promise was Isaac. . . . and the Lord confirmed those same promises to Isaac.

Paul (Galatians 3:16) declared that the Lord's promise to Abraham to bless all nations of the earth through his **"seed"** was a statement of the Gospel. That statement appeared early in the Old Testament. (Genesis 12:3) The **"seed"** of Abraham to whom this referred was the Son of God, Jesus Christ, who would be born into Abraham's family — and Isaac's family — but many, many years later!

The Lord made this same promise, a statement of the Gospel referencing his "**seed,**" to Isaac in Genesis 26:4.

The family of Abraham had become the Lord's chosen people! He would be their God, and they would be His people! The groundwork had been set for the Lord to have His desires: a people with whom He could fellowship, a people who would worship Him as God, and a people who would love Him!

Just as God was able to fellowship with Abraham throughout his life, He was able to fellowship with Isaac throughout his life also.

11

Isaac Wasn't Perfect Either

Isaac is also revered as one of the patriarchs. But lest anyone forgets, Isaac was a descendant of Adam, created in Adam's image and likeness. This means Isaac was a sinner, like all the rest of us. He was not perfect! . . . and God knew it!

Let's consider Isaac's walk before the Lord.

Abimelech, King of the Philistines

We have to look no further than to Isaac's actions when the famine hit the land in his day.

When a famine hit in Abraham's day, Abraham took his family to Egypt without first consulting the Lord. The Lord did not stop him. The Lord didn't make any comments for or against his trip. But the Lord watched over him, without interfering with his journey.

When a famine hit the land in Isaac's day, Isaac also intended to travel to Egypt until the famine was past. (Genesis 26:2) The first person Isaac approached for help was **not** the Lord, but Abimelech, king of the Philistines. (Genesis 26:1)

The first person Isaac should have consulted when he needed help and guidance was the Lord! . . . but he did not! Isaac was **not** relying on the Lord! Hadn't Isaac heard the Lord's promises to his father? . . . which included promises to Abraham's "**seed**"? . . . and to his own "**seed**"? One would think that when the God of heaven makes such promises to your family, the first person you would consult when problems arise would be the God of heaven! Go figure!

The Lord Gives His Counsel

This time, however, the Lord spoke up. He told Isaac to remain **"in the land,"** and He would be with him!

Having prevented Isaac and family from traveling to Egypt to ride out the famine, the Lord reconfirmed with Isaac the promises He had made to Abraham:

"Sojourn in this land, and I will be with thee, and will bless thee; for unto thee, and unto thy seed, I will give all these countries, and I will perform the oath which I sware unto Abraham thy father." (Genesis 26:3)

After hearing the Lord's words, Isaac and family didn't travel to Egypt. They remained in Gerar. (Genesis 26:6) That is, on this point Isaac listened to the Lord. . . . but it didn't take long before he went his own way again.

Isaac Lies About Rebekah

While they were dwelling in Gerar, Isaac had the same fear for his life because of his wife Rebekah as Abraham's fear for his life because of his wife Sarah. When the Philistines asked Isaac about Rebekah, he lied! He said she was his sister! She may have been a distant relative of his, but she certainly wasn't his sister. This wasn't a half-truth like when his father used the ploy — this was an outright lie!

Isaac should have consulted the Lord about this. Maybe he wasn't supposed to have moved to Gerar in the first place! Maybe the Lord had another solution for Isaac and family to endure the famine. . . . but Isaac never asked!

Without prompting from the Lord, Abimelech realized that Rebekah was Isaac's wife. Abimelech then charged all of his people to have nothing to do with Isaac and Rebekah because they were man and wife. When Abimelech issued this order to his people, he threatened death to any of them who disobeyed! (Genesis 26:11)

Had Isaac not been in Gerar, because he had first consulted the Lord, he might not have had to lie about his wife!

Summary

Isaac wasn't a terrible son of Abraham, but he was a descendant of Adam, and therefore he was a sinner, like his father.

The Lord promised to bless Isaac! He reaffirmed with Isaac all of the promises He had made to his father Abraham. But note: the Lord reaffirmed the promises to Isaac for **Abraham's** sake.

Isaac was the son of promise to his father, Abraham, and the Lord blessed him. Moses made no mention, however, of the faith of Isaac in these passages.

The line of Abraham continued through his son Isaac. The Lord made the same promises of innumerable descendants to Isaac, that He made to Abraham. The Lord was clear — He intended the descendants of Abraham and Isaac to be **His** people. . . . but Isaac's relationship with the Lord was not as strong as his father's!

If Isaac lived today, most people would consider him to be a 'good guy.' But he was a sinner in the line of Adam. . . . and the Lord knew it! Even so, the Lord chose **His** people to be of the "**seed**" of Isaac! They would be His people, and He would be their God!

The Line Continues to Jacob

Jacob, whose name the Lord changed to *Israel*, had twelve sons who became the heads of the twelve tribes of Israel, all members of whom were to become God's chosen people. All members of these twelve tribes are known to us collectively as **"the children of Israel."** These people were chosen by God to be His children on earth who would love, worship, and obey Him!

Let's consider the life of Jacob (Israel), the father of this great people, and the Lord's relationship with him.

Isaac Blessed Jacob as the Firstborn

Isaac had two sons — twins — named Esau and Jacob. Esau was the elder, Jacob the younger. . . . but one day, when Esau thought he was about to die of hunger, he sold Jacob his birthright for a bowl of *pottage* — a bowl of a thick stew.

The birthright meant nothing to Esau, which is why he so easily parted with it! . . . supposedly! As soon as he had eaten the pottage, however, Esau behaved as if he still possessed the birthright. So his sale of the birthright to Jacob for some food was a lie. In his mind, it never happened.

When it came time for Isaac to bless his firstborn, Esau was happily going to accept the blessing. Sold his birthright? No way!

In order to receive the blessing of the firstborn, Jacob and his mother Rebekah tricked his father Isaac. At that time, Isaac was almost blind. Because he could not see clearly to identify his son, he asked who it was who stood before him to receive the blessing of the firstborn. Disguised as his brother, Jacob lied to him and said, "**I am Esau thy firstborn.**" (Genesis 27:19) . . . and Isaac blessed him with the blessing of the firstborn.

Jacob lied to receive the blessing, and Isaac didn't check with God to determine who was standing before him. Isaac was tricked! . . . and Jacob received the blessing as the firstborn son of Isaac.

Isaac Blessed Jacob Again

At a later date, Isaac called Jacob before him and again gave him blessings from God:

"³**And God Almighty bless thee, and make thee fruitful, and multiply thee, that thou mayest be a multitude of people; ⁴and give thee the blessing of Abraham, to thee, and to thy seed with thee; that thou mayest inherit the land wherein thou art a stranger, which God gave unto Abraham.**" (Genesis 28:3-4)

Isaac was clear that God would bless Jacob. Isaac knew he had been blessed by the Lord God because of the Lord's relationship with his father, Abraham. Isaac also knew that the Lord was going to continue those blessings upon his son Jacob, and upon Jacob's descendants, for the same reason — because of the Lord's relationship with **Abraham.**

The Lord Blesses Jacob

When Jacob had his dream, known to us as the dream of *Jacob's Ladder*, he saw a ladder, most likely a giant staircase, which reached from earth to heaven. Jacob saw "**the angels of God ascending and descending on it.**" (Genesis 28:12)

In this dream, the Lord spoke to Jacob from the top of the ladder:

"¹³**And, behold, the LORD stood above it, and said, 'I am the LORD God of Abraham thy father, and the God of Isaac: the land whereon thou liest, to thee will I give it, and to thy seed; ¹⁴and thy seed shall be as the dust of the earth, and thou shalt spread abroad to the** west, and to the east, and to the north, and to the south: and in thee and in thy seed shall all the families of the earth be blessed. [15]And, behold, I am with thee, and will keep thee in all places whither thou goest, and will bring thee again into this land; for I will not leave thee, until I have done that which I have spoken to thee of." (Genesis 28:13-15)

The Lord promised to make Jacob's descendants as numerous as the dust of the earth. . . . and He would spread them all over the earth. He repeated His promise (vs 14) which Paul called the Gospel, that "**in thy <u>seed</u> shall all the families of the earth be blessed.**" This "seed" referred to Jesus, according to Paul.

The Lord also promised Jacob that He would be "**with thee,**" would "**keep thee,**" and would "**not leave thee,**" until all of His promises to Jacob had been fulfilled.

Jacob's Name Changed to "Israel"

The Lord then changed Jacob's name to *Israel. Jacob* means "He will supplant." (Newberry Bible, margin, Genesis 25:26) *Israel,* however, means "A Prince of God." (Newberry Bible, margin, Genesis 32:28)

The name *Jacob* had to do with his relationship to his brother Esau, whom he supplanted. The name *Israel* had to do with his relationship to the Lord God.

Throughout the Bible, Jacob is called by both names: Jacob and Israel. The two names may appear to be interchangeable, but they are not. When we see a reference to *Jacob*, it points to him acting on his own as a man, without consulting God. When we see a reference to *Israel*, it points to his relationship with God! Sometimes, he is called by both names in the same verse! We must read and consider each such verse carefully!

We see frequent references throughout the Bible to "**the children of Israel,**" which refers to Israel's many descendants in their status as people of God.

The man Israel had a special relationship to the Lord God! The man Israel was the father of the people whom the Lord had chosen to be His Own! Throughout Old Testament history, the Lord's chosen people on earth were known as "**the children of Israel.**" Clearly, not all of Jacob's descendants were actually children of God, but those who were children of God were also children of Israel (with rare exceptions, of course.)

God Repeats His Promises

God told Jacob to go to Bethel, to dwell there, and to make an altar there unto the Lord God. (Genesis 35:1) Jacob then moved his whole house to Bethel in obedience to the Lord. The altar that Jacob built there he called "**Elbethel**," which means "God of Beth Ēl" (Newberry Bible, margin, Genesis 35:7), and since *Bethel* means *house of God*, the name *Elbethel* means *God of the house of God*.

Then God spoke to Jacob again:

"¹⁰**And God said unto him, 'Thy name is Jacob: thy name shall not be called any more Jacob, but Israel shall be thy name:' and he called his name 'Israel.' ¹¹And God said unto him, 'I am God Almighty: be fruitful and multiply; a nation and a company of nations shall be of thee, and kings shall come out of thy loins; ¹²and the land which I gave Abraham and Isaac, to thee I will give it, and to thy seed after thee will I give the land.' "** (Genesis 35:10-12)

This was a confirmation to Israel of all the promises the Lord God had made to both Abraham and Isaac. The Lord promised to give the land of Canaan to Israel and to all of his descendants.

Israel was the father of the family the Lord God had chosen to be His People. The Lord was looking forward to having a big family of His Own on earth, of whom Israel was to be the head!

13

But Jacob Was A Sinner

It is clear that Jacob was not perfect. He was a descendant in the line of Adam as were his father Isaac and grandfather Abraham.

From all that we know of Jacob, he was a good man who enjoyed fellowship with God — even though he remained a sinful son of Adam.

The Lord gave Jacob and his boys and their descendants every opportunity to establish a close relationship with Him.

Jacob Lied to Obtain the Blessing for the Birthright

Jacob bought the birthright from his brother Esau with a bowl of pottage. This seems to have been an honest purchase transaction on his part. As soon as Esau had eaten the pottage, however, he acted like he had never sold the birthright. That attitude showed Esau was a dishonest man.

When it came time for Isaac to bless his firstborn son, it was clear that Esau intended to receive that blessing. Neither the birthright, nor the sale of his birthright, meant anything to Esau! . . . but the blessing of the firstborn was a big deal! . . . and Esau would gladly accept it!

Jacob and his mother Rebekah plotted to trick Isaac into blessing Jacob as his firstborn. Due to the transaction with Esau, the birthright should have been Jacob's, but he went about receiving the blessing in the wrong way. To receive this blessing, he behaved as a child of Adam, not a child of God. We do not read anywhere that Jacob took this issue before the Lord. He and his mother simply made immediate plans to trick his father!

Then, when Jacob was disguised to look, feel, and smell like Esau, and his nearly blind father Isaac asked if he really was his son Esau, Jacob answered, "**I am Esau thy firstborn.**" (Genesis 27:19) He lied!

Isaac wasn't convinced. He asked again, "**Art thou my very son Esau?**" and Jacob lied again, "**I am.**" (Genesis 27:24)

These two lies show Jacob to be a sinner in the line of Adam. This transaction clearly demonstrates that Jacob was a flawed individual! . . . and fellowship with God would be limited as a result.

Summary

The Lord promised to be with Jacob! . . . and going forward, Jacob would be known by the new name *Israel*, which means *Prince with God*.

Israel, grandson of Abraham, was the father of the Lord's people. They were, after all, known as the twelve tribes of **Israel**! The Lord promised to bless Israel's family and to make them innumerable on the earth!

Yet it is clear that Jacob was not perfect. Surely there are more sins of Jacob recorded in the Bible, but we only need to show these two lies to demonstrate the point. Jacob was a liar! He was flawed! He was a sinner! . . . as are we all!

God had chosen His people on earth to come from the stock of Abraham, Isaac, and Jacob. He gave them every opportunity to know Him, His power, and His capabilities, and to obey His commandments, His statutes, and His directives!

Because they all had free will, they all had every opportunity to choose for themselves whether or not they would serve the Lord. Jacob was willing to serve the Lord some of the time, but his sinful nature remained intact and controlled a lot of his behavior.

14

The Line Continues with the Children of Israel

Because Abraham believed God, the Lord chose him to be the patriarch of God's family on earth. The line of promise went from Abraham, to Isaac, to Jacob, and on to Jacob's children known as "**the children of Israel.**"

All of Jacob's children had to deal with indwelling sin. Neither Abraham, Isaac, nor Jacob were particularly bad men. All three of them obeyed the Lord when He gave them commands, and they did worship Him and fellowship with Him. But as we showed, all three of them had issues with sin.

All three of them would be rated by society as 'good men.' We wouldn't rate any of them as totally evil. Some of the kings of Judah and Israel whom we will be studying later deserved the descriptors *evil* and *wicked.* . . . but such terms didn't apply to the three patriarchs.

None of the three, however, were perfect. The Lord chose a line for His people on earth which, by necessity, ran through sinful men. The question was whether or not the three men believed God. Abraham believed God and God credited righteousness to his account. God extended His promises to Isaac and to Jacob, not because they believed God, but because Abraham did! It appears that Isaac and Israel **did** believe God, but Moses never specifically attributed belief to either of them.

Now we come to the children of Israel, the descendants of these men. How will they behave towards the Lord? Will they appreciate the special honor the Lord offered them to be His people on earth? We will examine this as our study continues.

The Family Moves to Egypt

During the great famine of the day, Jacob's son Joseph was in charge of all Egypt. Out of jealousy, Joseph's brothers had sold him into slavery. This showed very early in the story that the brothers had major problems with their sinful natures! To rid themselves of their brother Joseph, they discussed killing him. (Genesis 37:20) But they didn't do it; they sold him into slavery instead; and they lied about it to their father Jacob, suggesting that Joseph was dead — killed by a wild beast!

Joseph was rather obnoxious; the brothers were jealous; and it was no secret that Jacob was heavily biased towards Joseph, his favorite son. None of this facilitated smooth sailing within the family.

As a slave, Joseph ended up serving the Egyptian pharaoh. When Pharaoh had two dreams, Joseph, with the Lord's help, interpreted the dreams for him. The dreams indicated that 7 years of great plenty were coming to the land, to be followed immediately by a devastating 7-year famine. Pharaoh decided he needed to put someone in charge of the whole country to prepare and lead it through the famine. Because Pharaoh recognized that the Lord was with Joseph in everything he did, he chose Joseph to fill the role.

With the Lord's help during the seven years of plenty, Joseph harvested, collected, and stored huge quantities of grain in Pharaoh's warehouses! When the famine hit, Egypt was well-prepared!

Back in Canaan, Joseph's family was suffering food shortages from that same famine. They heard that Egypt had plenty of food stores, and so the brothers traveled to Egypt to purchase grain. They did not recognize Joseph as the man in charge because it had been many years since they had last seen him.

When they realized that their brother Joseph was in charge of the whole land of Egypt, Jacob and his family moved to Egypt to ride out the famine.

Years after the famine ended, Jacob, Joseph, Pharaoh, and all of Joseph's brothers had died. The whole family still lived in Egypt, but by then, a new Pharaoh, who did not know Joseph, had come into power.

During all those years in Egypt, the Lord had blessed the children of Israel! Their numbers had grown from 70, when Jacob first brought the family to Egypt, to a few million. Over those years, the children of Israel had gone from favored guests because of their relationship to Joseph, to slaves and brick makers for the Egyptians.

Because their numbers had grown and grown, the Egyptians began to fear the power of the Hebrew people.

"My People"

According to the book of Exodus, the Lord chose Moses and Aaron to lead the children of Israel out of slavery and out of Egypt.

What name did the Lord choose for the children of Israel? He sent Moses and Aaron before Pharaoh numerous times with the following message: **"Let My people go"**! According to the Lord, the children of Israel were **"My people."** He considered them to be His people — His children. . . . and He had Moses and Aaron repeat this exact demand numerous times to Pharaoh.

The Name of the Lord

The Lord told Moses:

"And I appeared unto Abraham, unto Isaac, and unto Jacob, by the name of God Almighty, but by My name Jehovah was I not known to them." (Exodus 6:3)

God Almighty is the translation of the Hebrew **"Ēl Shaddai."** (Newberry Bible, margin, Exodus 6:3) The Lord told Moses that Abraham, Isaac, and Jacob knew him as **"God Almighty"** — a name which speaks of God's omnipotence and demands fear and respect for His great power! The Lord wanted the people to know Him by His name **"Jehovah,"** however, which is a more personal name to be used among family members.

Jehovah means "He that is, and that was, and that is to come." (Newberry Bible, margin, Exodus 6:3) With respect to the name *Jehovah*, Vine wrote, "God chose it as His personal name by which He related specifically to His chosen or covenant people." (Vine's, p 140) Strong wrote that *Jehovah* means "(the) *self Existent* or eternal; *Jehovah*, Jewish national name of God." (Strong's)

The name *Jehovah*, often translated "**the LORD**," is used several thousand times throughout the Bible. But the Lord told Moses that Abraham, Isaac, and Jacob didn't know Him by that name. . . . and He wanted the children of Israel to learn to know Him by this new name — Jehovah.

The name *Jehovah* also causes us to look forward to the New Testament to God's Son, Jesus Christ. An angel of the Lord spoke to Joseph, betrothed of Mary, "[20] . . . **Joseph, thou son of David, fear not to take unto thee Mary thy wife: for that which is conceived in her is of the Holy Ghost.** [21]**And she shall bring forth a son, and thou shalt call His name JESUS: for He shall save His people from their sins.**" (Matthew 1:20-21)

Matthew explained that this was fulfillment of the prophecy in Isaiah 7:14, "**Therefore the Lord Himself shall give you a sign; 'Behold, a virgin shall conceive, and bear a son, and shall call His name Immanuel.' **" (Matthew 1:23)

The name *Jesus* means "Jehovah the Saviour." (Newberry Bible, margin, Matthew 1:21) The name *Immanuel* means "God with us." (Newberry Bible, margin, Isaiah 7:14)

The name *Jehovah*, by which the Lord wanted the children of Israel to know Him, relates closely to the name of His Son *Jesus* — that is, *Jehovah the Saviour*. Jesus of the New Testament was the fulfillment of a prophecy (Isaiah 7:14) wherein He, the Son of God, would also be known as "**Immanuel**" — *God with us*. *Jehovah the Saviour* was the "**prophet**" — the spokesman — God promised to raise up unto the people. (Deuteronomy 18:15)

All of these names are closely related. By wanting to be known as *Jehovah*, God was giving the children of Israel a taste of the close family relationship which was to come! . . . and which He greatly desired!

The Lord's Covenant with the Children of Israel

During their time in slavery, the Lord reminded the people that He remembered the covenant He made with their fathers! The Lord heard the groanings from their bondage in Egypt, and He remembered His covenant to give them the land of Canaan for ever!

"**⁴And I have also established My covenant with them, to give them the land of Canaan, the land of their pilgrimage, wherein they were strangers. ⁵And I have also heard the groaning of the children of Israel, whom the Egyptians keep in bondage; and I have remembered My covenant.**" (Exodus 6:4-5)

Having remembered the covenant He made with Abraham, Isaac, and Jacob, He sent Moses and Aaron to lead the children of Israel out of slavery in Egypt and back to the promised land of Canaan.

The Lord's Words to the People

The Lord told Moses to repeat His words to the children of Israel. Here, we see the Lord's goal for the children of Israel — He wanted them to be His people and He would be their God! He would rescue them, redeem them, give them the land of Canaan, and take them unto Himself for a people! "**. . . and I will be to you a God.**" Having done all of this, He was going to make sure that all of the children of Israel knew Him! They were all going to know that the Lord God of their fathers had done this for them!

"**⁶Wherefore say unto the children of Israel, 'I am the LORD, and I will bring you out from under the burdens of the Egyptians, and I will rid you out of their bondage, and I will redeem you with a stretched out arm, and with great judgments: ⁷and I will take you to Me for a people, and I will be to you a God: and ye shall know that I am the LORD your God, which bringeth you out from under the burdens of the Egyptians. ⁸And I will bring you in unto the land, concerning the which I did swear to give it to Abraham, to Isaac, and to Jacob; and I will give it you for an heritage: I am the LORD.'**" (Exodus 6:6-8)

We see in this passage the statement of the Lord's great desire for a people of His own. His people would be the children of Israel! He planned to bring them out of Egypt, rescue them out of bondage, redeem them, and take them unto Himself as a people! To what end? "**I will take you to Me for a people, and I will be to you a God.**" (vs 7)

The Lord wasn't doing this because of their stellar behavior (because their behavior was **not** stellar), but because of the promises He made to Abraham. Abraham believed God! . . . and God was doing all of this for the children of Israel because of His promises to Abraham.

The People Believed

When the Lord saved the children of Israel from the Egyptians by bringing them safely through the Red Sea, and by totally destroying the Egyptian army in the process, the people believed!

"And Israel saw that great work which the LORD did upon the Egyptians: and <u>the people</u> **feared the LORD, and** <u>believed the LORD,</u> **and His servant Moses."** (Exodus 14:31)

Having seen the mighty hand of the Lord in action after they walked through the Red Sea on dry land, and having seen the Egyptian armies engulfed by the waters and destroyed, the people **believed** the Lord! On this day, and at this time, the children of Israel believed! . . . but how quickly they would forget!

The Lord Sought Obedience

The Lord asked the children of Israel to obey His statutes, His judgments, and His commandments. Why? Throughout the books of Moses, we find quite a few reasons. If the people obeyed all of His words, He promised all of the following:

- **"I will put none of these diseases upon thee."** (Exodus 15:26)
- he **"shall live in them,"** (Leviticus 18:5)
- the land will **"spue not you out also."** (Leviticus 18:28)
- **"ye shall dwell in the land in safety."** (Leviticus 25:18)
- **"Then I will give you rain in due season, and"**
- **"the land shall yield her increase, and"**
- **"the trees of the field shall yield their fruit."** (Leviticus 26:5)
- **"And I will give peace in the land, and"**
- **"ye shall lie down, and"**
- **"none shall make you afraid; and"**
- **"I will rid evil beasts out of the land,"**
- **"neither shall the sword go through your land."**
     (Leviticus 26:6)
- **"And ye shall chase your enemies, and"**

- "they shall fall before you by the sword." (Leviticus 26:7)
- "And five of you shall chase an hundred, and"
- "an hundred of you shall put ten thousand to flight: and"
- "your enemies shall fall before you by the sword."
  (Leviticus 26:8)
- "For I will have respect unto you, and"
- I will "make you fruitful, and"
- I will "multiply you, and"
- I will "establish My covenant with you." (Leviticus 26:9)
- " And ye shall eat old store, and"
- ye shall "bring forth the old because of the new."
  (Leviticus 26:10)
- "And I will set My tabernacle among you: and"
- "My soul shall not abhor you." (Leviticus 26:11)
- "And I will walk among you, and"
- I "will be your God, and"
- "ye shall be My people." (Leviticus 26:12)
- "that ye may live, and"
- that ye may "go in and possess the land which
  the LORD God of your fathers giveth you."
  (Deuteronomy 4:1)
- "that ye might do them in the land whither ye go over
  to possess it." (Deuteronomy 4:14)
- "that it may go well with thee,
  and with thy children after thee, and"
- "that thou mayest prolong thy days upon the earth,
  which the LORD thy God giveth thee, for ever."
  (Deuteronomy 4:40)
- "that thy days may be prolonged." (Deuteronomy 6:2)
- "that it may be well with thee, and"
- "that thou mayest go in and possess the good land
  which the LORD sware unto thy fathers."
  (Deuteronomy 6:18)
- that ye may "fear the LORD our God, for our good always,"
- "that He might preserve us alive, as it is at this day."
  (Deuteronomy 6:24)

- "that the LORD thy God shall keep unto thee
    the covenant and the mercy which He sware
    unto thy fathers." (Deuteronomy 7:12)
- "And the LORD hath avouched thee this day to be
    His peculiar people, as He hath promised thee."
    (Deuteronomy 26:18)
- "And to make thee high above all nations
    which He hath made,
    ○ in praise, and
    ○ in name, and
    ○ in honour; and"
- "that thou mayest be an holy people unto the LORD
    thy God, as He hath spoken." (Deuteronomy 26:19)
- "And the LORD thy God will make thee plenteous
    in every work of thine hand . . . for good,
    ○ in the fruit of thy body, and
    ○ in the fruit of thy cattle, and
    ○ in the fruit of thy land." (Deuteronomy 30:9)
- "that thou mayest live and multiply: and"
- that "the LORD thy God shall bless thee in the land
    whither thou goest to possess it." (Deuteronomy 30:16)

The Lord agreed to keep all of these wonderful promises to the children of Israel if they simply obeyed Him. This is a magnificent array of promises He made to an especially privileged people. What did He want in return from them as their part in the bargain?

"[12]And now, Israel, what doth the LORD thy God require of thee, but to fear the LORD thy God, to walk in all His ways, and to love Him, and to serve the LORD thy God with all thy heart, and with all thy soul, [13]to keep the commandments of the LORD, and His statutes, which I command thee this day for thy good?" (Deuteronomy 10:12-13)

For their part, the Lord wanted the children of Israel . . .

- "to fear the LORD thy God,"
- "to walk in all His ways,"
- "to love Him,"
- "to serve the LORD thy God with all thy heart,"
- "to serve the LORD thy God . . . with all thy soul,"

- "to keep the commandments of the LORD," and
- "to keep . . . His statutes."

This seems to be a very reasonable request! He wanted the children of Israel to think of Him as their Father! He wanted the children of Israel to know Him as **Jehovah**, to be His people, and to obey Him. For doing so, He would be their God, He would care for them, and He would love them. (Exodus 6:7)

The Lord's Reason

When the Lord was giving His laws to the people through Moses, He explained His reasons for doing all this for the children of Israel. Everyone needs to read this passage very carefully because it says exactly what we have been attributing to the Lord as His reason for creating man. In this case, He declares His intentions to the children of Israel!

"⁶**For thou art an holy people unto the LORD thy God: the LORD thy God hath chosen thee** <u>to be a special people unto Himself, above all people that are upon the face of the earth.</u> ⁷**The LORD did not set His love upon you, nor choose you, because ye were more in number than any people; for ye were the fewest of all people:** ⁸**but** <u>because the LORD loved you,</u> **and because He would keep the oath which He had sworn unto your fathers, hath the LORD brought you out with a mighty hand, and redeemed you out of the house of bondmen, from the hand of Pharaoh king of Egypt.**

⁹**Know therefore that the LORD thy God, He is God, the faithful God, which keepeth covenant and mercy** <u>with them that love Him</u> **and keep His commandments to a thousand generations.**" (Deuteronomy 7:6-9)

Moses told the children of Israel that the Lord chose them "because the LORD loved you"! (vs 7) . . . and He was looking for their love and obedience in return! (vs 9) . . . to a thousand generations!

This is what the Lord wanted from all mankind! . . . and here, He stated it to His chosen people Israel! They would grow to be an innumerable people, and the Lord would have the fellowship He desired with them!

That was the plan!

15

But the Children
of Israel Rebelled

We have to go no further than to the words of Moses, just before his death, to see that the children of Israel were not living up to their part of the bargain.

"²⁷For <u>I know thy rebellion, and thy stiff neck</u>: behold, while I am yet alive with you this day, <u>ye have been rebellious against the LORD</u>; and how much more after my death?

²⁸Gather unto me all the elders of your tribes, and your officers, that I may speak these words in their ears, and call heaven and earth to record against them. ²⁹For I know that after my death ye will utterly corrupt yourselves, and turn aside from the way which I have commanded you; and evil will befall you in the latter days; because ye will do evil in the sight of the LORD, to provoke Him to anger through the work of your hands." (Deuteronomy 31:27-29)

The children of Israel rebelled against the Lord all throughout their days of wandering in the wilderness. During that time, they were known to complain, complain, complain about everything!

Moses described the people as having a "**stiff neck.**" He described them as being "**rebellious against the LORD.**" He expected their behavior to only worsen after his death! He said they would "**corrupt**" themselves, they would "**turn aside**" from the way he showed them, they would "**do evil in the sight of the LORD,**" and they would "**provoke Him to anger.**" He was right!

Moses wanted the elders and leaders of the children of Israel to gather so he could speak those words to them. Then, he blasted them!

This is pretty simple to explain. The children of Israel were all descendants of Adam.   The evils and corruptions which showed themselves immediately before the great flood of Noah's day, had manifested themselves again among the children of Israel.

The Lord had been totally gracious unto the children of Israel. He did everything for them! He rescued them from Egypt; He guided them through the wilderness; He fed them; He supplied them with water to drink; . . . and they repaid Him with rebellion and rejection.

The Lord's chosen people, with whom He wanted to have fellowship, were not appreciative of His love, His fellowship, nor His leadership! The children of Israel were all sinners, most of whom refused to admit having anything to do with sin! . . . and they did not feel the need for, nor did they want to be the Lord's children.

They wanted to live their lives on their own! They wanted to go their own way! . . . and they certainly didn't want any interference in their lives from God! . . . even if He was a loving God!

They were all representative of, and like, Adam and they showed it constantly! Even through all of this, the Lord continued to interact with the people. He did a lot for them for which they gave Him no credit, and showed no appreciation! Because they were paying so little attention to Him, they didn't know He was doing anything at all for them!

16

The Lord Appointed
Joshua to Lead the People

At the end of Deuteronomy, Moses died in the wilderness after being allowed to see the land of Canaan only from afar. The Lord then appointed Joshua to lead the children of Israel.

The Lord had promised Abraham, Isaac, and Jacob that He would give the land of Canaan to their descendants. That promise was about to be fulfilled.

Joshua Appointed

The Lord appointed Joshua to lead the people because Moses had sinned and was not allowed to lead the people across Jordan, neither was he allowed to even set foot in the promised land!

"**And the LORD said unto Moses, 'Behold, thy days approach that thou must die: call Joshua, and present yourselves in the Tabernacle of the congregation, that I may give him a charge. And Moses and Joshua went, and presented themselves in the Tabernacle of the congregation.'** " (Deuteronomy 31:14)

A few verses later, the Lord's words to Joshua are recorded:

"**And He gave Joshua the son of Nun a charge, and said, 'Be strong and of a good courage: for thou shalt bring the children of Israel into the land which I sware unto them: and I will be with thee.'** " (Deuteronomy 31:23)

91

Throughout the book of Joshua, we see the outworking of that charge to Joshua among the children of Israel.

Following the death of Moses, the Lord spoke these words to Joshua:

"Moses My servant is dead; now therefore arise, go over this Jordan, thou, and all this people, unto the land which I do give to them, even to the children of Israel." (Joshua 1:2)

Joshua began to lead the people from that moment forth. . . . and the people obeyed Joshua's commands:

"And they answered Joshua, saying, 'All that thou commandest us we will do, and whithersoever thou sendest us, we will go.' " (Joshua 1:16)

Their Passage Over Jordan

The day the children of Israel stood on the east side of Jordan, ready to pass over, the Lord told Joshua how he was to proceed:

"And the LORD said unto Joshua, 'This day will I begin to magnify thee in the sight of all Israel, that they may know that, as I was with Moses, so I will be with thee.' " (Joshua 3:7)

At the Lord's direction, Joshua told the priests who were carrying the ark of the covenant to step into the Jordan and then stand still with it. When they did so, **"the waters which came down from above stood and rose up upon an heap very far from the city Adam . . . and the people passed over right against Jericho."** (Joshua 3:16)

By following Joshua's directions, given to him by the Lord, the Jordan's waters stopped and the people walked across Jordan on dry ground.

"And the priests that bare the ark of the covenant of the LORD stood firm on dry ground in the midst of Jordan, and all the Israelites passed over on dry ground, until all the people were passed clean over Jordan." (Joshua 3:17)

After all the people had passed over Jordan, the Lord magnified Joshua in the people's eyes as promised:

"On that day the LORD magnified Joshua in the sight of all Israel; and they feared him, as they feared Moses, all the days of his life." (Joshua 4:14)

The people were off to a good start with Joshua in the lead.

The Taking of Jericho

When the children of Israel approached Jericho, the first city they encountered in the promised land, Joshua saw "**a man over against him with his sword drawn in his hand.**" (Joshua 5:13) Joshua approached him to learn if he was friend or foe.

"**And he said, 'Nay; but as captain of the host of the LORD am I now come.' And Joshua fell on his face to the earth, and did worship, and said unto him, 'What saith my lord unto his servant?'** " (Joshua 5:14)

This appears to have been the Lord Himself, "**captain of the host of the LORD,**" come down to help Joshua and the people against Jericho.

Everyone must admit that the taking of Jericho was **not** done through the great strength nor might of the army of the children of Israel, but by the great strength and miraculous hand of the Lord!

The Lord's instructions to Joshua were as follows:

"**³And ye shall compass the city, all ye men of war, and go round about the city once. Thus shalt thou do six days.**

⁴And seven priests shall bear before the ark seven trumpets of rams' horns: and the seventh day ye shall compass the city seven times, and the priests shall blow with the trumpets. ⁵And it shall come to pass, that when they make a long blast with the ram's horn, and when ye hear the sound of the trumpet, all the people shall shout with a great shout; and the wall of the city shall fall down flat, and the people shall ascend up every man straight before him." (Joshua 6:3-5)

This is not the normal way for an army to attack the great walls protecting a city. But the Lord commanded them to simply carry the ark of the covenant in a procession around the city, followed by the armies, once a day for six days. On the seventh day, the procession was to march around the city seven times, accompanied by the blasting of trumpets. Then, on command, all the people were to "**shout with a great shout,**" and the walls would "**fall down flat.**"

Had any of us been among the children of Israel that week, I'm sure our reactions to this would have been, "That's crazy!!" . . . and maybe the people did react that way, but they obeyed Joshua's commands from the Lord, and the walls fell down flat, just as the Lord said they would!

No matter how crazy this may have sounded, the people obeyed, the walls fell down, and they marched straight in, and took the city of Jericho!

"So the people shouted when the priests blew with the trumpets: and it came to pass, when the people heard the sound of the trumpet, and the people shouted with a great shout, that the wall fell down flat, so that the people went up into the city, every man straight before him, and they took the city." (Joshua 6:20)

The Lord told Joshua what he and the people were to do; Joshua relayed the Lord's instructions to the people; the people obeyed; the walls "came a tumblin' down"; and the people marched straight in and destroyed the city! Wherever each man stood in the line of march around the city, they simply turned to face the city center and marched straight in to the city — over and through the rubble which had once been walls!

The People's Resolve

As recorded in the book of Joshua, the Lord guided the people through the promised land while He gave many nations and peoples into their hands. Then, Joshua oversaw the distribution of the lands to the people as their inheritances from the Lord.

Near the end of Joshua's life, he called the people together and presented them with a message from the Lord. This included the Lord's words (vs 13), as well as Joshua's own advice to the people (vss 14-15):

"13And I have given you a land for which ye did not labour, and cities which ye built not, and ye dwell in them; of the vineyards and oliveyards which ye planted not do ye eat.

14Now therefore fear the LORD, and serve Him in sincerity and in truth: and put away the gods which your fathers served on the other side of the flood, and in Egypt; and serve ye the LORD.

15And if it seem evil unto you to serve the LORD, choose you this day whom ye will serve; whether the gods which your fathers served that were on the other side of the flood, or the gods of the Amorites, in whose land ye dwell: but as for me and my house, we will serve the LORD." (Joshua 24:13-15)

This last verse (vs 15) is a famous quotation from the lips of Joshua. **"As for me and my house, we will serve the LORD."**

Notice from the admonitions of Joshua in verses 14-15 that other gods and idols still remained among the people. They were a constant temptation to the children of Israel. Not only had some of those gods come from before the flood, and from their days of slavery in Egypt, but many such gods were worshipped by the people of the promised land, whom they were to have destroyed. Many idols were still in the people's possession where they remained constant temptations to lead them away from the Lord.

The people answered Joshua with these words:

"**[16]And the people answered and said, 'God forbid that we should forsake the LORD, to serve other gods; [17]for the LORD our God, He it is that brought us up and our fathers out of the land of Egypt, from the house of bondage, and which did those great signs in our sight, and preserved us in all the way wherein we went, and among all the people through whom we passed: [18]and the LORD drave out from before us all the people, even the Amorites which dwelt in the land: therefore will we also serve the LORD; for He is our God.**" (Joshua 24:16-18)

This sounds good! Right? The people seemed to understand the Lord! . . . but they didn't understand themselves very well. These were good words! . . . but Joshua warned them that if they didn't obey the Lord as they said they would, "**. . . then He will turn and do you hurt, and consume you, after that He hath done you good.**" (Joshua 24:20)

The people maintained their resolve: "**And the people said unto Joshua, 'Nay; but we will serve the LORD.'**" (Joshua 24:21)

Summary

That conversation between Joshua and the people ended with the people making a covenant in which they resolved to serve the Lord.

"**[22]And Joshua said unto the people, 'Ye are witnesses against yourselves that ye have chosen you the LORD, to serve Him.' And they said, 'We are witnesses.'**

[23]'Now therefore put away,' said he, 'the strange gods which are among you, and incline your heart unto the LORD God of Israel.'

[24]And the people said unto Joshua, 'The LORD our God will we serve, and His voice will we obey.'

²⁵**So Joshua made a covenant with the people that day, and set them a statute and an ordinance in Shechem."** (Joshua 24:22-25)

Joshua wrote their covenant in the book of the law so they would remember it.

Whoever finished the book of Joshua wrote this comment at the end of the book:

"And Israel served the LORD all the days of Joshua, and all the days of the elders that overlived Joshua, and which had known all the works of the LORD, that He had done for Israel." (Joshua 24:31)

As we have seen and will continue to see, under strong leadership, such as Moses and Joshua, the tendency of the people to forget the Lord and worship idols was kept in check. During the days of Joshua and the elders who served with him, the people served the Lord. They looked like they were going to fulfill the Lord's desire for the children of Israel to be His people.

But the Children of Israel
Sinned During Joshua's Life

Judging by Joshua's comments at the end of his life, he knew the children of Israel were going to have trouble obeying the Lord. He especially knew they would struggle with all the heathen gods and idols in their midst.

We see the results of these foreseen problems during the days of the judges. But during the days of Joshua's leadership, the children of Israel had to learn the hard way to trust the Lord.

The Children Sinned with Respect to Jericho

When the city of Jericho was destroyed, Joshua warned the children of Israel to stay away from **"the accursed thing."** This referred to any of the spoil related to heathen gods which they would find in the city. Just to have such objects in one's possession was abomination unto the Lord! All such objects were to be totally destroyed! . . . and the people were to have nothing to do with them!

"And ye, in any wise keep yourselves from the accursed thing, lest ye make yourselves accursed, when ye take of the accursed thing, and make the camp of Israel a curse, and trouble it." (Joshua 6:18)

Looking ahead to the next chapter, we see: **"But the children of Israel committed a trespass in the accursed thing: for Achan, the son of Carmi, the son of Zabdi, the son of Zerah, of the tribe of Judah, took of**

the accursed thing: and the anger of the LORD was kindled against the children of Israel." (Joshua 7:1)

The children of Israel had kindled **"the anger of the LORD"** because one of them had taken forbidden spoil from Jericho.

The children of Israel were all descendants of Adam, and as such, they all struggled with indwelling sin. The sin, which dwelt in their hearts, kept them at odds with the Lord God!

Notice also in this case that the sin of only one man kindled the anger of the Lord against the whole people! Numerous children of Israel were **not** involved. It was only one man! . . . but one was enough!

The Conquest of Ai

For another example of the attitudes of the children of Israel, we need to look no further than the very next city the people approached after the destruction of Jericho: the city of Ai.

The city of Jericho was destroyed through the great power of the Lord. No one can march around a city's walls, sound trumpets, shout, and cause the walls to crumble! No one! . . . except the Lord God! He was responsible for the 'easy' conquest of Jericho!

The People Attacked Ai Without Consulting the Lord

The people seemed to think that Jericho was destroyed because of their great and wonderful skills as warriors! They seemed to think they were indestructible! . . . and they didn't need the Lord!

So they moved on from Jericho to scout the city of Ai. The scouts returned to Joshua and reported that Ai would be easy to take! They would only need to use a few thousand warriors.

As a result, the children of Israel sent 3000 warriors against Ai. But they didn't consult the Lord. Even if they had, He was ignoring them until the issue of **"the accursed thing"** was resolved. Since they didn't check with the Lord, they didn't know He was not with them.

When the 3000 men went up against Ai, they were overwhelmed and severely smitten. The men of Ai chased the warriors of Israel back towards Jericho and smote them as they fled! This **"melted"** the hearts of the children of Israel.

Joshua even tore his clothes, "**fell to the earth upon his face before the ark of the LORD**," and put dust upon his head. (Joshua 7:6) These were signs of deep sorrow and anguish. Then, he cried unto the Lord — and He blamed the loss on the Lord!

The Lord told him to get up and asked why he was lying on his face? (Joshua 7:10) Then, the Lord said:

"**Israel hath sinned, and they have also transgressed My covenant which I commanded them: for they have even taken of the accursed thing, and have also stolen, and dissembled also, and they have put it even among their own stuff.**" (Joshua 7:11)

The Lord explained that "**the children of Israel could not stand before their enemies, but turned their backs before their enemies, because they were accursed: neither will I be with you any more, except ye destroy the accursed thing from among you.**" (Joshua 7:12)

The Lord was angry with the children of Israel and He was going to destroy the guilty person(s). The next morning, they identified the person to be of "**the family of Judah,**" of "**the Zarhites,**" and of the family of "**Zabdi.**" Out of that family, they identified "**Achan.**" (Joshua 7:17-19)

As it turns out, Achan had taken "**a goodly Babylonish garment,**" of the spoils of Jericho, as well as silver and gold. He admitted, "**they are hid in the earth in the midst of my tent, and the silver under it.**" (Joshua 7:21)

They recovered the spoils and destroyed them, along with Achan, his family, and all his possessions. (Joshua 7:23-25)

Then, and only then, do we read that "**the LORD turned from the fierceness of His anger.**" (Joshua 7:26)

The Lord Sends Them Against Ai

When the problem of Achan and "**the accursed thing**" had been resolved, the Lord told Joshua to send the armies of the children of Israel against Ai. One might think they would be hesitant to attack Ai again, but this time, the Lord told them to do it. The Lord said, "**see, I have given into thy hand the king of Ai, and his people, and his city, and his land.**" (Joshua 8:1)

There was a great difference between the two attacks: when they attacked Ai the first time, the Lord had not directed them to attack, and

He was not with them. In fact, because they hadn't consulted Him, they didn't know He was angry with them. But the second time, the Lord was with them, and He said He had given Ai into their hands.

The second time, Joshua chose 30,000 warriors and sent them out that night to take up ambush positions **behind** the city of Ai. (Joshua 8:3-4)

The first time they attacked Ai directly with only 3000 men. The warriors of Ai came out of the city, chased the men of Israel back towards Jericho, and smote them as they fled. The second time, Joshua and his army would approach the city directly again. When the army of Ai came out against them, they would turn and run back toward Jericho, just as the 3000 did the first time. This would draw the army of Ai out of their city.

This time, however, when the army of Ai came forth to chase the children of Israel, the large ambush force would attack from its cover, take, and burn the empty city! **"Then ye shall rise up from the ambush, and seize upon the city: for the LORD your God will deliver it into your hand."** (Joshua 8:7)

The next morning Joshua led his army towards Ai. When the armies of Ai came out to repel their attack, everyone with Joshua turned and ran back towards Jericho. All the men of the city of Ai **"pursued after Israel."** (vs 17) The Lord then told Joshua to signal the army which was lying in ambush! Those troops lying in ambush attacked the city of Ai and set it afire! No men remained behind in Ai to defend the city, so it was an easy target to take, destroy, and burn.

When the army of Israel was finished and the whole city of Ai was in flames, the large force came forth behind the army of Ai. . . . and when they did, the army with Joshua stopped and turned back to face their pursuers. The army of Ai was totally destroyed from before and behind! They were trapped! . . . and they were wiped out!

The point to note here is that when the Lord is behind one's efforts, anything is possible! To go it alone, as the children of Israel tried to do the first time, brought prompt defeat! The second time, with the Lord in charge, the children of Israel were victorious!

Summary

The people of Israel agreed to serve the Lord, but they demonstrated that they were quick to go it alone without checking with the Lord first. *Going your own way* is the definition of *iniquity*.

These two actions (taking and hiding **"the accursed thing,"** and attacking Ai without explicit instructions from the Lord) demonstrated once again that all of Israel were descendants of Adam! . . . and that fact prevented the Lord from having close fellowship with this people whom He had chosen to be His own.

He still desired to be their God, and He still wanted them to be His people, but He was dealing with a stubborn, stiff-necked, and sinful people of Israel who wanted nothing to do with Him!

True fellowship would continue to be minimal at best! A few individuals here or there wanted to fellowship with the Lord, but the people as a whole stood aloof of His every effort!

18

A New Start
with Judges

Joshua led the children of Israel into the promised land. As they moved through the land, the children of Israel were supposed to throw the nations out of the land, or they were to destroy them outright! But many times, they simply did not obey!

The children of Israel took many of the people of the land into their number as servants. One nation tricked them into making a peace treaty which brought that whole nation among the children of Israel. The Lord God did not want any of this to happen. But the people disobeyed His directions!

A Cycle Begins

As long as there was a strong leader at the head of the children of Israel, like Moses and Joshua who were faithful to the Lord God of Israel, the people worshipped the Lord. The people followed such leaders reluctantly, but they followed.

"And the people served the LORD all the days of Joshua, and all the days of the elders that outlived Joshua, who had seen all the great works of the LORD, that He did for Israel." (Judges 2:7)

As soon as a strong leader died, however, the children of Israel rebelled against the Lord and went their own way.

After the death of Moses, the Lord's choice to lead the people into the promised land was Joshua. Joshua was appointed immediately upon Moses' death, so there was no gap in leadership at that time.

When Joshua, and the elders of his day, died, however, we read this:

"**[11]And the children of Israel did evil in the sight of the LORD, and served Baalim: [12]and they forsook the LORD God of their fathers, which brought them out of the land of Egypt, and followed other gods, of the gods of the people that were round about them, and bowed themselves unto them, and provoked the LORD to anger. [13]And they forsook the LORD, and served Baal and Ashtaroth.**" (Judges 2:11-13)

While the people were ignoring the Lord and worshipping idols, the Lord "**sold them into the hands of their enemies round about.**" (Judges 2:14)

When the people became greatly distressed (vs 15), the Lord established a new judge (a new leader) to deliver them from their enemies and return them to the land! (vs 16)

Here is the cycle:

- under a strong leader (judge) the people worshipped the Lord,
- when the judge died, the people returned to their idols,
- after a while, when the Lord's anger was sufficiently kindled,
    He gave the people into the hands of an enemy,
- when the people became distressed by their captivity
    and called upon the Lord to save them,
    He sent a new judge to rescue them,
- and a new cycle began.

That was the cycle. The people's relationship with the Lord went up, down, up, down, etc., through quite a few cycles.

Without a strong leader, every one of the children of Israel did that which was right in their own eyes — which meant they rebelled against the Lord. It wasn't that the people became strong when a judge was in charge. The people were just as rebellious, but the strength of personality and leadership of the judge, plus the fact that the Lord guided, supported, and empowered the judge, drew the people to the Lord.

It was a herd mentality, however! Wherever the leader led, the people would follow. Remove the leader, and the people scattered — each in his or her own direction!

This was the nature of the period of the judges.

Some Specific Judges

Gideon

Let's look at Gideon as an example.

"**And the children of Israel did evil in the sight of the LORD: and the LORD delivered them into the hand of Midian seven years.**" (Judges 6:1)

"**When the children of Israel cried unto the Lord because of the Midianites,**" the Lord sent a prophet who told them they had not obeyed the Lord. (Judges 6:7-10)

Then, the Lord appointed Gideon to rescue the people. An angel of the Lord came to Gideon and said, "**The LORD is with thee, thou mighty man of valour.**" (Judges 6:12) The Lord told Gideon that he was going to save the children of Israel from the Midianites "**as one man.**" (Judges 6:16)

Gideon wanted a sign from the Lord to show that the Lord was really with him. The angel gave him a sign (Judges 6:21), and he was satisfied. Then, the Lord spoke again directly to Gideon:

"**And the LORD said unto him, 'Peace be unto thee; fear not: thou shalt not die.'** " (Judges 6:23)

The Altar of Baal

The Lord followed this greeting with some new marching orders:

"[25]**And it came to pass the same night, that the LORD said unto him, 'Take thy father's young bullock, even the second bullock of seven years old, and throw down the altar of Baal that thy father hath, and cut down the grove that is by it:** [26]**and build an altar unto the LORD thy God upon the top of this rock, in the ordered place, and take the second bullock, and offer a burnt sacrifice with the wood of the grove which thou shalt cut down.**" (Judges 6:25-26)

Gideon did as the Lord requested. The people of the city were upset! They wanted to kill Gideon! . . . but Gideon's father, Joash, told them that the insult was against Baal — **"Let him plead for himself."** (Judges 6:31) . . . but Baal said nothing.

Gideon's Fleece

The Lord then told Gideon that he was going to send him to save Israel from the Midianite armies. Gideon wasn't so sure about this. The Lord would save Israel by Gideon's hand?? Really?? Gideon requested a sign — his famous fleece — so the Lord could verify to Gideon that He really meant what He said!

Gideon took a fleece of wool, placed it on the ground, and asked the Lord — if He really intended to save Israel by Gideon's hand — to soak the fleece with dew, but not the ground around it. Early the next morning, he found it to be so. The fleece was soaked, the ground was dry. (Judges 6:36-38)

Then Gideon pleaded with God that He not be angry, but he wanted to see another sign. This time, he requested the fleece be dry and the ground be wet. The next morning, it was so! (Judges 6:39-40)

The Lord meant what He said! . . . and Gideon was satisfied!

The Battle Against the Midianites

When it came time to battle the host of Midian, Gideon gathered the armies of Israel. The Lord told Gideon that his 32,000 warriors were **too many**. (Judges 7:2)

How can there ever be too many warriors in an army?   Right?? . . . but the Lord told Gideon he didn't need so many warriors.

First, Gideon allowed everyone who was **"fearful and afraid"** to depart. Of his army, 22,000 departed which left him with 10,000 warriors. The Lord said that number was still **too large**! (Judges 7:3-4)

This time, Gideon brought the warriors down to water and told them to drink. Those who lapped up the water with their tongues, as dogs do, were told to depart. Those who lifted water to their mouths with their cupped hands were allowed to remain. This narrowed the number of Gideon's army to 300, which was a good number according to the Lord. (Judges 7:5-7)

How large was the Midianite army? They were **"as grasshoppers for multitude, for both they and their camels were without number."** (Judges 6:5)

The Lord would deliver the Midianite army into Gideon's hand with only 300 men! That night, Gideon divided the men into three companies. He gave each man a trumpet, a pitcher, and a lamp. (Judges 7:16)

Gideon and his men spread out and surrounded the camp of the Midianites. Each man had a lamp concealed within his pitcher. On Gideon's signal, the men blew their trumpets, broke their pitchers exposing their lamps, waved their lamps around, and shouted, **"The sword of the LORD, and of Gideon."** (Judges 7:19-20) They made such a ruckus surrounding the camp that it caused confusion and chaos within the camp! The Midianites thought they were surrounded; in their scramble to escape, confusion ensued; and the Midianites killed each other with their own swords. (Judges 7:21-22)

Those Midianites who remained after the melee were easily destroyed by the army of Israel. The Lord gave Gideon and his 300 men the victory against the Midianites, Amalekites, and all the other children of the east who were camped in that valley. Note again the number disparity: the Midianites and company were **"like grasshoppers for multitude; and . . . as the sand by the sea side for multitude."** (Judges 7:12) . . . and Gideon with his 300 men, under the Lord's command, were victorious!

This is why the leaders of Israel never needed to number their troops! When the Lord was with them, numbers didn't matter! They could have great victories with only a handful of men! The magnificent size of the Israelite army was meaningless when the Lord was in charge!

Samson

Samson was another judge of the people of Israel. He is rather famous, as biblical judges go, but he seemed to **not** take his position very seriously.

"And the children of Israel did evil again in the sight of the LORD; and the LORD delivered them into the hand of the Philistines forty years." (Judges 13:1)

The children of Israel had been at a low point in one of their cycles; they had done evil; and the Lord handed them over to the Philistines.

At that same time, the Lord promised a son to Manoah and his wife (who had been barren.) This was to be a special child, whom they would name Samson:

"**³And the angel of the LORD appeared unto the woman, and said unto her, 'Behold now, thou art barren, and bearest not: but thou shalt conceive, and bear a son. ⁴Now therefore beware, I pray thee, and drink not wine nor strong drink, and eat not any unclean thing: ⁵for, lo, thou shalt conceive, and bear a son; and no razor shall come on his head: for the child shall be a Nazarite unto God from the womb: and he shall begin to deliver Israel out of the hand of the Philistines.' "** (Judges 13:3-5)

The Lord was going to raise up this child to be a judge who would rescue Israel from the Philistines and rule Israel for 20 years.

Samson's first wife was a Philistine woman. (Judges 14:7-10) Samson was known to be a very strong man, and when necessary, the Lord helped him to be even stronger.

When a lion roared and attacked him, he destroyed the lion with his bare hands:

"**And the Spirit of the LORD came mightily upon him, and he rent him as he would have rent a kid, and he had nothing in his hand . . .**" (Judges 14:6)

Later, Samson offered the people a riddle related to that event. If the people solved the riddle, he would reward them. The Philistines co-opted Samson's wife to attempt to learn the secret of the riddle. . . . and Samson played along with them! He didn't sound very serious about his service to the Lord. To him, the riddle and its solution were parts of a big game!

Eventually, he lost this challenge, because he told his wife the answer to the riddle, and she immediately passed the information along to the Philistines. Then, **"the Spirit of the LORD came upon him"** to help him make the payment he owed for losing the challenge. (Judges 14:19)

After this loss, they gave his wife to another man. When Samson learned of it, he burned the Philistines' fields. In retribution for the loss of their fields, the Philistines killed his wife and her father. Samson then avenged their deaths by smiting the Philistines with "**a great slaughter.**" (Judges 15:8)

When the Philistines sent a large force to Judah to smite Samson, the men of Judah handed Samson over to the Philistines. But "**the Spirit of the LORD came mightily upon him,**" he burst his cords and killed 1000 Philistines with "**a new jawbone of an ass.**" (Judges 15:14-15)

Later, Samson fell in love with a woman named Delilah. (Judges 16:4) She conspired with the Philistines to learn the secret of his great strength. This, too, was a game she played, and he played right along. He made up several false explanations for his great strength. He should have known they meant to harm him if they could learn his secret. . . . but Samson continued to treat it as a game.

One night, "**he told her all his heart.**" (Judges 16:17) This time, he told Delilah **the truth.** He told her that if he cut off his hair, he would have no strength. She immediately passed that news along to the Philistines. That night, they shaved his head; he lost his strength; they took him captive; and they put out his eyes! (Judges 16:21) The 'game' ended with Samson a blind captive!

Days later, the Philistines threw a great party to offer sacrifices to their god Dagon. They brought the blind Samson to the party as entertainment. They chained him between two great pillars which held up the building. By this time, Samson's hair was beginning to return.

Samson prayed to the Lord to give him strength one last time:

"**O Lord GOD, remember me, I pray thee, and strengthen me, I pray thee, only this once, O God, that I may be at once avenged of the Philistines for my two eyes.**" (Judges 16:28)

The Lord granted this request. With all his might, Samson brought down the two great pillars which held up the whole house. It came down upon him and all of the Philistines at the party. In addition to Samson, a large number of Philistines died that day!

The Lord used Samson to rescue the people from the Philistines. When the Lord was with Samson, he wielded great power! When the Lord was not with Samson, and when his hair was cut, however, he was weak!

So as we see throughout the book of Judges, whenever the people needed to be rescued from an oppressor, the Lord sent a judge to rescue them! . . . and when the judges ruled, the people behaved properly towards the Lord.

The Lord could find some fellowship when the judges reigned, but generally speaking, fellowship with the people in those days was scarce to non-existent.

The cycle, however, continued!

19

When the Judges Died,
the People Sinned

The Cycle

When the Lord placed a judge in power, the people behaved themselves (somewhat). After a judge died, however, the people reverted to normal form — and they went back to worshipping idols.

Up, down, up, down, up, down . . . the cycle continued.

The End State

When the time of the judges neared its end, which is recorded towards the end of the book of Judges, we read the following statement (which appears twice):

"In those days there was no king in Israel, but every man did that which was right in his own eyes." (Judges 17:6)

The Lord had given the children of Israel judges to rule over them, but the people were not happy with that arrangement. When the people did evil, the Lord gave them into the hands of their enemies. . . . and more and more, the people simply did whatever they wanted to do — regardless what the Lord had to say.

Doing that which is right in one's own eyes is the definition of *iniquity*.

. . . and without a king or a strong leader, increasing iniquity leads to anarchy!

False Religious Practices

The story in Judges 17, tells of a man named Micah, who was a thief. Micah had stolen 1100 shekels of silver from his own mother. That was a lot of money! She demonstrated she was a lousy mother because she was okay with his thievery. In fact, when he gave the money back to her, she used it to purchase **"a graven image and a molten image"** for him — for her son the thief! (Judges 17:4)

The mother put the new images in Micah's house, which was **"an house of gods."** (Judges 17:5) Then, Micah made himself a religious garment — an ephod — and other items to resemble those used in the Tabernacle; he hired a Levite to be his priest; and he set up his own **false** religion in his house!

Micah's religious practices, vessels, and trappings resembled the practices, vessels, and trappings of Judaism, but overall, Micah's self-designed religious practices were but a reasonable facsimile of Judaism. Micah believed that outward appearances alone define a religion: **"Now know I that the LORD will do me good, seeing I have a Levite to my priest."** (Judges 17:13) He thought all he needed was a Levite, and trappings similar to those used in Judaism, and he could set up his own house of worship! He thought he was all set because his religious practices looked identical to Judaism — except the God of Judaism was not participating in his false religious practices. It may have looked like Judaism, acted like Judaism, and sounded like Judaism, but the Lord God was absent from it and it was all **phony**!

It is amazing that anyone could set up **their own** religion which follows **their own** rules, and still believe the Lord has a part in it!

This is what we see today throughout 21st Century society. People use the Lord's name for all manner of statements, and they think because they say the words "the Lord," frequently, He is actually doing whatever it is they suggest He is doing. They think that because their actions mimic real worship, they have the real thing! . . . without ever inviting the Lord Himself to participate!

They use phony religious practices which lead men, women, and children away from the Lord! They use the Lord's name frequently; they use religious garments which look real; and they build extravagant palaces of worship! So it sounds real, looks real, feels real . . . and totally impresses mankind! . . . except, as we've said, it's totally **phony**! Yet many are convinced that the Lord blesses such efforts.

This example, recorded in Judges 17, happened almost 3500 years ago, but this type of phony religious behavior is still among us and going strong today!

The Lord wanted a people of His own with whom He could fellowship, love, and dwell. The Lord explained in great detail, through Moses, the practices the people were to follow to worship Him. But by the end of the time of the judges, the people were setting up their own idols and images and inventing their own false religions and religious practices. Outwardly, this may have looked like they were worshipping the One True God, but inwardly, they were seeking self-gratification! Such phony religious practices have absolutely nothing to do with the Lord!

The message these people propound is that all roads lead to the Lord! They tell their followers, "Worship however you want, and the Lord will bless your efforts."

In reality, the Lord has nothing to do with phony religious practices! Those who want to worship the Lord must do so according to the Lord's instructions — not according to the imaginations of mankind.

During the time of the judges, the people demonstrated that they were struggling with indwelling sin! . . . and it was winning! Not only were the world, the flesh, and the devil helping to win the battle with sin, but the people were actively rejecting and ignoring the One True God who could actually have helped! This is particularly sad!

The very last verse of the book of Judges again clearly identifies the state of the children of Israel in those days:

"In those days there was no king in Israel: every man did that which was right in his own eyes." (Judges 21:25)

The Lord's goals for mankind had not changed, but during the time of the judges, the fulfillment of those goals was far removed from ever happening! Nevertheless, the Lord continued to work to draw the people to Him!

A New Start:
God Gave Israel A King

The children of Israel had the best possible leadership of any of the nations in the world. They had the Lord God of the universe who wanted them to be His children, wanted to take care of them, wanted to fellowship with them, wanted to love them, etc! It doesn't get any better than that!

But the children of Israel did not appreciate Him, nor did they want His interference in their lives! It was a shame, but that was their attitude. They rejected His advice, ignored His words, refused His instructions, and resisted His commands. . . . and these were descendants of Abraham — the very ones He chose to be His people — who were doing this!

When their society had deteriorated to the point we saw at the end of the book of Judges, where everyone did that which was right in their own eyes, anarchy reigned! Their society was a disaster!

Even worse, as we discussed, they had begun to invent their own religious practices which outwardly looked like the practices the Lord gave them to follow, but were totally foreign to Him.

They were doing exactly what Paul warned against: **"Having a form of godliness, but denying the power thereof . . ."** (2 Timothy 3:5)

As religious beings, mankind have the need to worship. Out of stubbornness, the children of Israel chose to worship gods invented by their own imaginations. They may have thought their gods resembled the God of the universe, but they did not! When the choice is between the

Lord God of the universe, who interacts with you and who actually wants your worship, adoration, love, and praise, and an inanimate object, which is totally incapable of thought, emotions, and actions, the right choice is pretty clear!

The behavior of the children of Israel was totally insulting to God!!

A King

When the people weren't pleased with judges, they raised their voices to call for a king. Why? They wanted to be like the other nations around them which were governed by kings. Their neighbor nations should have been envious of the children of Israel and the relationship they enjoyed with the God of the universe. Why? . . . because God was performing every function which the children of Israel sought in a king! . . . but rather, the children of Israel were envious of the neighbor nations and their human kings. Go figure!

The people expressed their desire for a king to the prophet Samuel. They said to him, "**Give us a king to judge us.**" (1 Samuel 8:6) Samuel understood the relationship to the Lord God which the people were fooling away. Samuel was greatly upset by this demand, and he immediately prayed to the Lord about it.

Samuel thought that the people's demand for a king was a rejection of **his** service to them. . . . but the Lord explained the real meaning of their demand: they were not rejecting Samuel — they were rejecting **the Lord!**

"**And the LORD said unto Samuel, 'Hearken unto the voice of the people in all that they say unto thee: for they have not rejected thee, but they have rejected Me, that I should not reign over them.' "** (1 Samuel 8:7)

The people's demand was a clear rejection of God's reign over them. We see this same attitude in the New Testament when the people refused to have Jesus, King of the Jews, to reign over them.

The Lord wanted Samuel to explain to them — to "**protest solemnly unto them**" (1 Samuel 8:9) — exactly how a human king would behave towards his people! (1 Samuel 8:11-18)

Samuel didn't paint a pretty picture of the attitudes and treatment of a human king toward his people, but the people rejected his warnings.

"[19]Nevertheless the people refused to obey the voice of Samuel; and they said, 'Nay; but we will have a king over us; [20]that we also may be like all the nations; and that our king may judge us, and go out before us, and fight our battles.' " (1 Samuel 8:19-20)

The Lord God wanted to care for the children of Israel as a Father cares for His children. The Lord **was** going out before them, fighting their battles, and doing exactly what they wanted a king to do for them! . . . but they didn't appreciate the Lord's efforts! . . . and regardless of Samuel's warnings, they still wanted a human king!

Finally, the Lord told Samuel to give them what they wanted: **"Make them a king."** (1 Samuel 8:22)

The Lord had told the people, through Moses, that if they demanded a king to reign over them, **"the LORD thy God shall choose"** the person who would reign. (Deuteronomy 17:15) The people would not be allowed to choose. God would choose!

So the Lord chose Saul to be their king.

Saul, Israel's First King

Samuel repeated the Lord's words unto the people. He declared that the Lord had **"saved you out of all your adversities and your tribulations."** Those were exactly the kinds of deeds the people expected of a king! Nevertheless, they refused God's care! So God called for them to present themselves before Him.

"And ye have this day rejected your God, who Himself saved you out of all your adversities and your tribulations; and ye have said unto him, 'Nay, but set a king over us.' Now therefore present yourselves before the LORD by your tribes, and by your thousands." (1 Samuel 10:19)

All the tribes of Israel came before the Lord. The Lord chose the tribe of Benjamin, and out of it He chose the family of Matri, and out of that family, He chose Saul, son of Kish.

"And Samuel said to all the people, 'See ye him whom the LORD hath chosen, that there is none like him among all the people?' And all the people shouted, and said, 'God save the king.' " (1 Samuel 10:24)

What description do we find of this new king?   Here is a description:

"**And he [Kish] had a son, whose name was Saul, a choice young man, and a goodly: and there was not among the children of Israel a goodlier person than he: from his shoulders and upward he was higher than any of the people.**" (1 Samuel 9:2)

Saul was a tall, handsome, goodly man!   When it was time to celebrate Saul's reign, we read:

"**And all the people went to Gilgal; and there they made Saul king before the LORD in Gilgal; and there they sacrificed sacrifices of peace offerings before the LORD; and there Saul and all the men of Israel rejoiced greatly.**" (1 Samuel 11:15)

Saul was king in Israel and everyone was happy!   The people had received their desire: a king!   They made him king "**before the LORD.**" . . . and they rejoiced greatly!

21

But King Saul Sinned

The Lord gave the children of Israel their desire: a king. But Samuel, the prophet of God, characterized that desire as "**wickedness.**" Clearly, the Lord was upset about having been rejected by His chosen people.

Samuel told the people, "**Is it not wheat harvest to day? I will call unto the LORD, and He shall send thunder and rain; that ye may perceive and see that your wickedness is great, which ye have done in the sight of the LORD, in asking you a king.**" (1 Samuel 12:17)

The Lord made His displeasure known to the people by sending thunder and rain during harvest season. Samuel declared that by these acts of the Lord, the people could "**perceive and see that your wickedness is great.**" Having heard this, the people feared the Lord.

Samuel told them that they did not need to fear the Lord. If they were obedient unto the Lord, the Lord would not forsake them, because He had chosen them to be His people. Even after the Lord was rejected by the people, if they obeyed Him, He would "**not forsake**" them. The Lord still wanted the children of Israel to be His people!

"**[20]And Samuel said unto the people, 'Fear not: ye have done all this wickedness: yet turn not aside from following the LORD, but serve the LORD with all your heart; [21]and turn ye not aside: for then should ye go after vain things, which cannot profit nor deliver; for they are vain. [22]For the LORD will not forsake His people for His great name's sake: because it hath pleased the LORD to make you His people.'**" (1 Samuel 12:20-22)

The Lord was giving the children of Israel every chance to turn unto Him! When He gave the people a king, the Lord's desire was for the king to lead the people to Him. That is why the Lord was looking for a king who was a man after God's own heart. This required that the king be willing to obey the Lord and look to Him constantly for counsel and leadership.

If the king and the people refused to obey the Lord, there would be consequences. Samuel warned, **"if ye shall still do wickedly, ye shall be consumed, both ye and your king."** (1 Samuel 12:25)

Eventually, that is exactly what happened. The king and the people behaved wickedly, and both the king and the people were consumed!

Saul's Sin

On one occasion, the Lord spoke to Saul through Samuel. Saul was told to wait at Gilgal for seven days until Samuel came. Then, Samuel would offer sacrifices and tell Saul what the Lord wanted him to do next. (1 Samuel 10:8)

But Saul was impatient! Samuel didn't arrive soon enough, so **Saul** offered his own burnt offering! It was not Saul's place to do that! Immediately after Saul made the offering, Samuel arrived.

When asked by Samuel, **"What hast thou done?"** Saul gave his excuses: Samuel hadn't yet come — he was late; the people were beginning to scatter; and the Philistines were assembling against him. He said he wanted to offer a sacrifice unto the Lord before the Philistines attacked. (1 Samuel 13:11-12) . . . so he went ahead and offered the sacrifice without waiting for Samuel.

Saul was not relying on the Lord. He was impatient, worried, headstrong, and relying on his own faulty reasoning. If he trusted that the Lord knew what was happening, he had no reason for any of his excuses! This shows that Saul really didn't trust the Lord! . . . and Samuel rebuked Saul for his behavior:

"¹³And Samuel said to Saul, 'Thou hast done foolishly: thou hast not kept the commandment of the LORD thy God, which he commanded thee: for now would the LORD have established thy kingdom upon Israel for ever. ¹⁴But now thy kingdom shall not

continue: the LORD hath sought Him a man after His own heart, and the LORD hath commanded him to be captain over His people, because thou hast not kept that which the LORD commanded thee." (1 Samuel 13:13-14)

Because Saul disobeyed, the Lord sought another king — He **"sought Him a man after His own heart,"** which was David, son of Jesse. David would be the next king of Israel! . . . and David **was** a man after God's own heart! (Acts 13:22)

When Saul next asked counsel of the Lord, the Lord did not answer. (1 Samuel 14:37) On that occasion, Saul had issued a stupid order; his son Jonathan was not present to hear the order; so without knowing he was doing so, Jonathan disobeyed the order; and Saul wanted to put him to death for his disobedience. The Lord had actually used Jonathan during that time to save the people, but that didn't matter to Saul. Saul was a proud man who had issued an order which his son Jonathan had disobeyed! It didn't matter to Saul whether Jonathan knew of the order — or not! Saul had issued an order! **. . . and he intended to carry it out!!** . . . and his son Jonathan was going to pay for his disobedience!

The fact that Saul's order meant death to his own son — so be it! Saul didn't care! He was king! He had spoken! Period! He showed he was a real sweetheart! He allowed his pride to take priority over his love for his own son!

But the people refused to help Saul! They stood their ground! In fact, **"the people rescued Jonathan, that he died not."** (1 Samuel 14:45)

Saul's pride had taken over, and he was not following the Lord's guidance. Samuel said as much:

"16And Samuel said unto Saul, 'Stay, and I will tell thee what the LORD hath said to me this night.' And he said unto him, 'Say on.' 17And Samuel said, 'When thou wast little in thine own sight, wast thou not made the head of the tribes of Israel, and the LORD anointed thee king over Israel?' " (1 Samuel 15:16-17)

"19'Wherefore then didst thou not obey the voice of the LORD, but didst fly upon the spoil, and didst evil in the sight of the LORD?' " (1 Samuel 15:19)

"22And Samuel said, 'Hath the LORD as great delight in burnt offerings and sacrifices, as in obeying the voice of the LORD? Behold,

to obey is better than sacrifice, and to hearken than the fat of rams.
[23]For rebellion is as the sin of witchcraft, and stubbornness is as iniquity
and idolatry. Because thou hast rejected the word of the LORD, he hath
also rejected thee from being king.'

[24]And Saul said unto Samuel, 'I have sinned: for I have
transgressed the commandment of the LORD, and thy words: because
I feared the people, and obeyed their voice.' " (1 Samuel 15:22-24)

The Lord said that when Saul was **little** in his own eyes, he was
made king. But as king, Saul allowed his pride to get the better of him; he
thought very highly of himself; he operated apart from the Lord; and that
was evil in the Lord's eyes!

Notice here that Saul didn't blame his sins on his own pride – he
blamed his sins on his fear of the people! . . . but actually, Saul really
didn't do much, if anything, out of fear for the people. He was king! He
did as he wanted! . . . and if the people didn't like it (or the Lord, for that
matter), too bad!

Then, Samuel emphasized (and this is good for all of us to know)
that **God prefers obedience rather than sacrifices and offerings**.

Saul had been told to wait for Samuel to offer sacrifices. Due to
impatience, he did not obey that instruction! Instead, Saul personally
offered sacrifices to the Lord, which was not his place to do! Saul
rationalized that offering sacrifices to the Lord trumped obedience, but
Samuel informed him that his reasoning was incorrect!

The Lord puts great value in **obedience**! . . . and later, we learn
that the Lord didn't really want sacrifices and offerings **at all**. "**In burnt
offerings and sacrifices for sin Thou hast had no pleasure.**" (Hebrews
10:6)

The Lord commanded sacrifices and offerings be made for sin so
the people would learn the price necessary to cover sins. . . . but the Lord
had no desire for the deaths of innocent beings! He much preferred
obedience! So Saul's reasoning was totally off base!

According to the Lord, "**rebellion is as the sin of witchcraft.**" .
. . and "**stubbornness is as iniquity and idolatry.**" (1 Samuel 15:23) By
doing all of these deeds independently of the Lord, Saul had rebelled! .
. . and for that, God **rejected him** from being king.

Finally, Saul admitted he had sinned – but in doing so, he blamed
it on the people! He said it was their fault! He refused to take full credit

for his own sins. The people and the circumstances had caused him to sin! That was just baloney! . . . and Saul knew it!

The Lord didn't immediately take the kingdom away from Saul. But the Lord did rather quickly anoint a new person to be king in Saul's place! The Lord chose David, son of Jesse, to be the next king. The Lord waited, however, until after the death of Saul before he crowned David king.

Saul demonstrated that he, as a descendant of Adam, had a real struggle with indwelling sin! The real fellowship, and the caring Father/son relationship, which the Lord desired to have with him and with the children of Israel, was again put on hold! Rather than being a good example of a man of God to the people, Saul set a terrible example! He showed them how they should **not** behave!

A New Start
with King David

Almost immediately after telling Saul that God had rejected him as king, the Lord sent Samuel to anoint His new choice for king out of the family of Jesse.

Samuel was afraid Saul would kill him if he learned of this task, but the Lord gave Samuel instructions, and Samuel obeyed.

The Sons of Jesse

Samuel traveled to Bethlehem to the house of Jesse to find the Lord's choice for king. Samuel told the elders of Bethlehem that he had come "**peaceably**" to sacrifice unto the Lord. Then, he invited Jesse and his sons to the sacrifice. (1 Samuel 16:5)

One by one, Jesse's sons passed before Samuel, and the Lord did not choose any of them. Then, Samuel asked Jesse if he had any more sons. He admitted that his youngest son, David, a shepherd, was tending his flocks. Samuel told Jesse to send for him.

"**And he sent, and brought him in. Now he was ruddy, and withal of a beautiful countenance, and goodly to look to. And the LORD said, 'Arise, anoint him: for this is he.'**" (1 Samuel 16:12)

"**Then Samuel took the horn of oil, and anointed him in the midst of his brethren: and the Spirit of the LORD came upon David from that day forward.**" (1 Samuel 16:13)

Not only did Samuel anoint David with oil, but "**the Spirit of the LORD came upon David from that day forward.**" As this verse teaches, the Spirit of the Lord indwelt David for the rest of his life. . . . and David was a man after God's own heart! It was a great relationship!

Here was a man with whom the Lord could (and did) have fellowship! David fully appreciated the Lord God of Israel!

King David

This is important! We reiterate: the Spirit of the Lord came upon David on the day on which he was anointed! . . . and the Lord was with David all the rest of his life. For that time in Old Testament history, this was a unique relationship. It was a taste of the relationship between New Testament believers and the Spirit of God! How did David walk before the Lord?

"**Because David did that which was right in the eyes of the LORD, and turned not aside from any thing that He commanded him all the days of his life, save only in the matter of Uriah the Hittite.**" (1 Kings 15:5)

We may wonder sometimes, throughout David's life, if he was behaving as the Lord desired. . . . but this verse from 1 Kings explains! **The Lord was with David all the rest of his life** — except on the occasion of his sin against Uriah, husband of Bathsheba.

The Lord testified later: "**I have found David the son of Jesse, a man after mine own heart, which shall fulfil all My will.**" (Acts 13:22)

David, being a man after God's own heart, was a person with whom the Lord God could fellowship and with whom He could have the Father/son relationship He desired!

The Lord sent His words to David through Nathan the prophet. The Lord spoke the following words of David's son, house, kingdom, and throne:

"**[15]But My mercy shall not depart away from him** [Solomon], **as I took it from Saul, whom I put away before thee** [David]. **[16]And thine house and thy kingdom shall be established for ever before thee: thy throne shall be established for ever.**" (2 Samuel 7:15-16)

The Lord's relationship with king David was as close a relationship as we find in the Bible — other than the relationship between God the Father and His Son.

We need to remember that Jesus Christ, Son of God, son of Mary, was born a man **of the house of David**! (Matthew 1:1) Jesus Christ, King of the Jews, is the King who fulfilled the prophecies we read in 2 Samuel 7:16. David's kingdom, house, and throne **have been** established "**for ever**" in the Person of the King — Jesus Christ. The promises the Lord made to David have been fulfilled!

23

But David Sinned

As we saw, David was a great king and a man after God's own heart! But David was a sinner, who had to deal with indwelling sin inherited from Adam, just like every other man and woman in this world!

Not only did David sin, but when it came to "**the matter of Uriah**" and Uriah's wife Bathsheba, David's sins were real whoppers!

According to 1 Kings 15:5, this was the major sin in David's life:

"**Because David did that which was right in the eyes of the LORD and turned not aside from any thing that He commanded him all the days of his life, <u>save only in the matter of Uriah the Hittite</u>.**"

The Spirit of the Lord may have been with David all of his life following his anointing, but David sinned against Uriah without any input from the Lord! That is, in the matter of Uriah, David totally ignored the Lord and succumbed to the temptations of the world, the flesh, and the devil all on his own!

Bathsheba

What had David done? He was at home, sleeping in the afternoon and early evening, when he should have been out with his troops in battle.

"**And it came to pass in the eveningtide, that David arose from off his bed, and walked upon the roof of the king's house: and from the roof he saw a woman washing herself; and the woman was very beautiful to look upon.**" (2 Samuel 11:2)

David should **not** have been sleeping in the late afternoon, because verse 1 described it as "**the time when kings go forth to battle.**"

Neither should he have been watching this woman bathe. To make matters worse, he enquired of her, and had her brought to him. Then, he lay with her, and she conceived.

Uriah

When David learned that Bathsheba was pregnant, he sent to the front for her warrior husband Uriah, enquired of him how the battle was going, and sent him home to his wife. But Uriah did not go home to Bathsheba. Had he done so, Uriah might have provided David some cover for his sin, but he did not. Had he gone in unto his wife, Bathsheba could have claimed the baby was his. But Uriah felt guilty that all the other warriors were out on the battlefield. Should he enjoy the luxury of sleeping at home with his wife while all his fellow warriors were at camp preparing for battle? He decided: No! . . . and he refused to go home to Bathsheba.

David tried again the next night, even going so far that time as to getting Uriah drunk. Then, he sent him home. Again, Uriah refused to go to his wife.

To solve the problem, David sent to Joab, his commander in the field, and ordered him to assign Uriah to the most intense part of the battle. He even explained to Joab that he wanted that Uriah **"may be smitten, and die."** (2 Samuel 11:15)

This was a terrible sequence of events for a man of God like king David. But he was guilty of all of this: he had ignored God in favor of his own evil reasoning!

Later, Joab sent a messenger to David to tell him that Uriah had been killed in battle. When Bathsheba learned of her husband's death, she mourned!

The Lord's Response

When the time of mourning was past, David brought Bathsheba into his house, and **"she became his wife, and bare him a son."** There is a **"But . . ."** coming: **"But the thing that David had done displeased the LORD."** (2 Samuel 11:27)

The Lord sent Nathan the prophet to speak with David. Nathan told David a story about a rich man who took terrible advantage of a poor man by killing his beloved pet lamb. This whole story can be found in 2 Samuel 12. David was so upset and angry over the story that he proclaimed to Nathan, "**As the LORD liveth, the man that hath done this thing shall surely die.**" (2 Samuel 12:5)

David added, "**And he shall restore the lamb fourfold, because he did this thing, and because he had no pity.**" (2 Samuel 12:6)

Nathan then declared to David, "**Thou art the man.**" (2 Samuel 12:7)

The Lord's angry words to David included, "**Wherefore hast thou despised the commandment of the LORD, to do evil in His sight?**" (2 Samuel 12:9) "**Now therefore the sword shall never depart from thine house; because thou hast despised Me, and hast taken the wife of Uriah the Hittite to be thy wife.**" (2 Samuel 12:10) "**Behold, I will raise up evil against thee out of thine own house . . .**" (2 Samuel 12:11) "**Howbeit, because by this deed thou hast given great occasion to the enemies of the LORD to blaspheme, the child also that is born unto thee shall surely die.**" (2 Samuel 12:13)

This one deed of David's was a great sin!   . . . and it had enormous consequences which affected David, Bathsheba, Uriah, the child, and three more of David's sons.

David told Nathan that the perpetrator of the evil deed in his story should repay "**fourfold.**" David ultimately paid with four of his own sons! The son born to Bathsheba (2 Samuel 12:18) died after seven days. Three more of David's sons, Amnon (2 Samuel 13:28-29), Absalom (2 Samuel 18:14), and Adonijah (1 Kings 2:25), also met with untimely deaths.

Plus, this affair really disrupted David's relationship with the Lord God!

David admitted sinning against the Lord. (Psalm 51) His sin was far-reaching. Not only did he sin against the Lord, but he sinned against Bathsheba, against Uriah, against his own children, and against his people!

Many of our sins seem minor to us, but they frequently are far-reaching, producing major consequences which affect many more people than just ourselves! . . . and they especially have negative effects on our relationship with the Lord.

As we know, David walked with the Lord most of his life, but a sin like this, for a descendant of Adam, should not be any surprise to anyone.

Note the Lord's description of David's sin: He said that David **"despised the commandment of the Lord,"** and he **"despised Me."** (2 Samuel 12:9-10) That's not good when the Lord credits anyone with despising Him!

David had directly caused the death of one of his men, so by the Mosaic law, he should have died. Nathan, however, told him that **"The LORD also hath put away thy sin; thou shalt not die."** (2 Samuel 12:13) David was guilty of this sin, but he would not be put to death — the Lord had **"put away"** the sin. David did, however, repay **"fourfold,"** just as David told Nathan the rich man in his story should pay: David lost four sons!

That fact that the Lord **"hath put away thy sin,"** shows that the Lord had a plan which would allow Him to forgive mankind's sins. David's Psalms indicate he understood God was going to do this!

This act of forgiveness to David is a sign to all of us that God was preparing to solve the sin problem! Let us be clear: no man was ever going to solve the sin problem on their own; God Himself was going to solve it! . . . and forgiveness would be offered to all mankind as a result of God's solution!

A Glorious Start
with King Solomon

When king David was near death, he named Solomon to reign next. What was Solomon's relationship with the Lord? **"And Solomon loved the LORD, walking in the statutes of David his father . . ."** (1 Kings 3:3) Solomon, too, was a man of God!

Conversation with the Lord

Upon being crowned king, the Lord spoke to Solomon:
"In Gibeon the LORD appeared to Solomon in a dream by night: and God said, 'Ask what I shall give thee.' " (1 Kings 3:5)

The Lord asked Solomon what He could do for him. Here was Solomon's answer:

"Give therefore Thy servant an understanding heart to judge Thy people, that I may discern between good and bad: for who is able to judge this Thy so great a people?" (1 Kings 3:9)

This was a very humble request which pleased the Lord. (1 Kings 3:10) In response to this, the Lord fulfilled Solomon's request — and He gave him a whole lot more!

"¹¹And God said unto him, 'Because thou hast asked this thing, and hast not asked for thyself long life; neither hast asked riches for thyself, nor hast asked the life of thine enemies; but has asked for thyself understanding to discern judgment; ¹²behold, I have done according to thy words: lo, I have given thee a wise and an understanding heart; so

that there was none like thee before thee, neither after thee shall any arise like unto thee. [13]And I have also given thee that which thou hast not asked, both riches, and honour: so that there shall not be any among the kings like unto thee all thy days.' " (1 Kings 3:11-13)

The Lord blessed Solomon in a mighty way. He gave him the wisdom and understanding which he requested, but He also gave him riches and honor! Solomon's kingdom flourished!

The Queen of Sheba

When the queen of Sheba came to visit to assess Solomon's kingdom, she was totally impressed! She had heard great things about Solomon which she didn't believe could be true. So she came to see for herself.

"[6]And she said to the king, 'It was a true report that I heard in mine own land of thy acts and of thy wisdom. [7]Howbeit I believed not the words, until I came, and mine eyes had seen it: and, behold, the half was not told me: thy wisdom and prosperity exceedeth the fame which I heard." (1 Kings 10:7-8)

The queen of Sheba recognized that Solomon's people were happy with his reign! She even recognized that the Lord was delighted in Solomon and that "the LORD loved Israel for ever." Solomon's testimony before the watching world was quite wonderful! ... and surely, that meant fellowship between the Lord, Solomon, and his people was quite wonderful as well! Here are the queen of Sheba's words:

"[8]Happy are thy men, happy are these thy servants, which stand continually before thee, and that hear thy wisdom. [9]Blessed be the LORD thy God, which delighted in thee, to set thee on the throne of Israel: because the LORD loved Israel for ever, therefore made He thee king, to do judgment and justice." (1 Kings 10:8-9)

Solomon did have a wonderful relationship with the Lord. The Lord said this about Solomon: "He shall be my son, and I will be his father; and I will establish the throne of his kingdom over Israel for ever." (1 Chronicles 22:10) Solomon was David's son, but the Lord treated Solomon as His own son!

The Lord had identified, in Solomon, one of the descendants of Adam with whom He could enjoy warm fellowship.

25

But Solomon Sinned

The Lord blessed Solomon in many ways, but Solomon was not perfect! . . . and we see that in the waning years of his life. As great as Solomon's early life was with respect to his obedience to, and fellowship with, the Lord, the end of his life was the totally opposite in character!

Solomon's Love for Women

Solomon may have been the wisest man on earth, but Solomon had a vast love for women — many "**strange**" women — as the KJV says. The word "**strange**," in this context means "foreign," (Strong's) as the whole of this first verse explains.

"**¹But king Solomon loved many strange women, together with the daughter of Pharaoh, women of the Moabites, Ammonites, Edomites, Zidonians, and Hittites; ²of the nations concerning which the LORD said unto the children of Israel, 'Ye shall not go in to them, neither shall they come in unto you: for surely they will turn away your heart after their gods: Solomon clave unto these in love.' "** (1 Kings 11:1-2)

As the author explained in verse 2, the children of Israel were not supposed to marry foreign women because they would bring their idols and gods into camp and into their houses, and that would cause the men of Israel to stray from their worship of the Lord God of Israel.

Solomon broke this rule many times. He had 700 wives and 300 concubines, "**and his wives turned away his heart.**" (1 Kings 11:3)

Solomon's many foreign wives did exactly what the Lord had warned the children of Israel they would do. They turned his heart away from the Lord God — and he began to worship heathen gods!

Solomon's Worship of Heathen Gods

Note the very next verses:

"⁴**For it came to pass, when Solomon was old, that his wives turned away his heart after other gods: and his heart was not perfect with the LORD his God, as was the heart of David his father. ⁵For Solomon went after Ashtoreth the goddess of the Zidonians, and after Milcom the abomination of the Ammonites. ⁶And Solomon did evil in the sight of the LORD, and went not fully after the LORD, as did David his father.**" (1 Kings 11:4-6)

"**When Solomon was old,**" he did evil before the Lord. In his old age, Solomon demonstrated that he was a descendant of Adam by straying from a wonderful relationship with the Lord!

The years of his old age could have been a wonderful time of fellowship between the Lord and Solomon, but it was ruined by Solomon's love for foreign women, and his acceptance and worship of their heathen gods (like the two mentioned in verse 5.)

The Lord had chosen the children of Israel to be His people, and out of those people, He selected David who was a man after His own heart! The Lord chose to establish the line of David's kingdom for ever! . . . and Solomon was born in that line! . . . but for all the great things Solomon did, and the close fellowship he enjoyed with the Lord, all of that changed as he neared the end of his life. Then, he led the children of Israel away from the Lord.

We see that described as doing "**evil in the sight of the LORD.**" This shows the frailties of the human body and the human mind as a person ages. This again can be credited to the consequences of Adam's sin. . . . and such frailty and deterioration can easily disrupt one's relationship with the Lord — as it did in Solomon's life!

Having observed Solomon's life, none of us dares ever presume to be free of all effects of fallen man! If we manage to miss senility and dementia in our old age, we can count that as a blessing from the Lord!

Hezekiah Was
A Good King

There were a number of good kings who followed after David and Solomon in the line of the kings of Judah. But the nation split into the kingdoms of Judah and Israel (all tribes of Israel but Judah) after Solomon's death. All future kings of Israel and some future kings of Judah were evil kings. Only a few kings in the line of David and Solomon were good kings.

According to Matthew 1:10, Hezekiah was the 10th king of Judah in the line of king David. Hezekiah was a particularly good king. During his lifetime, Hezekiah had to deal with the Assyrians and their king Sennacherib.

Hezekiah Cleaned Up the Land

There were many "**high places**" in the land which were sites of idol worship remaining from the heathen practices of the people of Canaan. Several of the kings of Judah cleaned out the idols and stopped the worship of heathen gods, but most of them left the high places intact. The children of Israel then began to worship in those high places.

As mentioned, Hezekiah was a good king. "**And he did that which was right in the sight of the LORD, according to all that David his father did.**" (2 Kings 18:3) Note that Hezekiah was a great, great, . . . , great grandson of David, but as a descendant in the line of David,

Hezekiah is credited with doing right before the Lord as **"David his father did."**

What exactly did he do to set himself apart?

Hezekiah Removed the Idols

"He removed the high places, and brake the images, and cut down the groves, and brake in pieces the brasen serpent that Moses had made: for unto those days the children of Israel did burn incense to it: and he called it Nehushtan." (2 Kings 18:4)

Hezekiah was the first of the kings to remove the **"high places."** Up to this point, the kings before Hezekiah did **not** remove the high places; the people built high places in all cities; and the kings and children of Israel burned incense to the Lord in the high places. The significance of the high places was that the people of **"every nation made gods of their own, and put them in the houses of the high places."** (2 Kings 17:29) The children of Israel associated high places with worship of any and all gods. Even though the Lord God was angered by this practice, the high places remained until Hezekiah became king.

"Images" were idols. **"Groves"** were not groves of trees as we understand the word today, but carved wooden idols. Hezekiah broke the images and cut down the idols which were the central focus of heathen worship.

Then we come to **"the brasen serpent that Moses had made."** This had been a solution to a specific problem in Moses' day, and it was a figure of the solution to the sin problem which indwells all mankind.

The problem in Moses' day was that poisonous snakes were biting the people, and people were dying. The Lord told Moses to construct the brazen serpent and mount it atop a tall pole. When bitten by a snake, the person merely had to look upon the brazen serpent atop the pole and they would live. They simply had to look upon the symbol of the problem — and they would live.

Mankind's problem (since Adam) has always been indwelling sin. The Lord Jesus hung atop the cross of Calvary where He was made sin for us. Anyone who looks upon Him on the cross, in faith, can have their sin problem resolved, and they can live! . . . eternally!

In both cases, the people had to have faith that the solution of looking up at a symbol of the problem could cure the problem. It wasn't that there was anything special about the piece of brass atop the rod. What was special was that the people were told that **looking** upon it would cure the problem. They had to have **faith** that the solution would work! They had to have faith to look up at the symbol!

That is similar to the sin problem and the cross of Christ! Each person has to have **faith** to cause them to look up at Christ on the cross! Many simply refuse to do that! It sounds too easy! . . . or it's too preposterous! How could something as simple as that really work?

If a person takes a skeptical attitude like that, and refuses to look to Jesus to solve the sin problem, that person will remain in their sins. . . . and there is no other solution to the sin problem! Working hard to overcome sin is not the solution! It requires **faith** that the identified solution — to look up to Jesus Christ, who was made sin for us as He hung on the cross — will actually work! . . . and it does!

Back to the brass serpent — in the years since that problem, the people had made an idol out of it. They began to burn incense to the brass image as if it could hear them and solve their problems. The serpent was called "**Nehushtan**" which appropriately meant "Piece of brass." (Newberry Bible, margin, 2 Kings 18:4)

That's all it was! . . . a piece of brass — an inanimate object! It was not a living, thinking, caring being. It was a piece of brass. So how could it help anybody in any way? It couldn't! . . . and it didn't! The action that worked in years past, was **to believe** that merely to look upon it would solve the problem of a serpent bite!

In the days since that problem, the people lost the significance of the piece of brass, and made it into an idol! The people treated it like a god who needed to be appeased and who would appreciate the care, worship, and adoration people showed it. That is just not possible from an inanimate object. Inanimate objects appreciate nothing! Pieces of brass appreciate nothing!

Hezekiah rightly understood it to be but a piece of brass, and he destroyed it!

Hezekiah Trusted the Lord God of Israel

Cleaning up the land was a help to the people. By doing so, and through his other actions, Hezekiah set a great example for the people.

"He trusted in the LORD God of Israel . . ." (2 Kings 18:5) **"For he clave to the LORD, and departed not from following Him, but kept His commandments, which the LORD commanded Moses."** (2 Kings 18:6)

How did the Lord treat Hezekiah? **"And the LORD was with him; and He prospered whithersoever he went forth: and he rebelled against the king of Assyria, and served him not."** (2 Kings 18:7) The Lord was with Hezekiah, and Hezekiah knew it! So when he could have crumbled and been forced to serve the king of Assyria, he refused! He continued to look to the Lord for guidance!

Hezekiah Dealt with Sennacherib

When Sennacherib, king of Assyria, sent his armies against Jerusalem and Judah, Hezekiah cooperated up to a point. When Sennacherib demanded tribute be paid, Hezekiah paid.

But when Sennacherib threatened the people of Judah through his boisterous spokesman Rabshakeh, Hezekiah did not cooperate. Rabshakeh told the people of Judah not to listen to Hezekiah when he told them that the Lord would save them. (2 Kings 18:29-30) Three times, Rabshakeh told the people of Judah to **"hearken not"** to Hezekiah. (2 Kings 18:31, 32)

Rabshakeh warned Hezekiah to not be deceived by his God: **"Let not thy God in whom thou trustest deceive thee, saying, 'Jerusalem shall not be delivered into the hand of the king of Assyria.' "** (2 Kings 19:10)

Rabshakeh threatened Hezekiah and the people of Judah with all manner of evil, crude, and disgusting punishments! His threats were accompanied by all manner of arrogance and braggadocio!

According to Rabshakeh, the Assyrians were really great, mighty, and powerful! No one could possibly stand up to them! . . . and if Hezekiah and the people of Judah didn't listen to him, they would pay dearly! Ultimately, after imposing severe punishments on the people of

Judah, and after the children of Israel succumbed to terrible punishments, Rabshakeh said they would be carted off into captivity in Assyria.

Rabshakeh did not trust the gods of Canaan, and he lumped the Lord God of Israel into a category with all other gods (except his own) — which have no powers at all! Rabshakeh put total trust, however, in the mighty power of his king Sennacherib! . . . and Sennacherib worshipped the god Nisroch!

Almost immediately after hearing Rabshakeh's latest threat, Hezekiah consulted with the Lord God through Isaiah the prophet. The Lord sent this message to Hezekiah regarding Rabshakeh and his armies: **"Behold, I will send a blast upon him, and he shall hear a rumour, and shall return to his own land; and I will cause him to fall by the sword in his own land."** (2 Kings 19:7)

Hezekiah prayed to the Lord for help, and the Lord sent word that He was sending help!

What was this **"blast"** mentioned in verse 7? In one night, when the Assyrians were encamped nearby preparing to battle the children of Judah, **"the angel of the LORD went out, and smote in the camp of the Assyrians an hundred fourscore and five thousand: and when they arose early in the morning, behold, they were all dead corpses."** (2 Kings 18:35)

Note: **one** angel of the Lord killed 185,000 warriors of Assyria in **one** night! **One** angel!

So much for the mighty power of Sennacherib's army! So much for the mighty power of Sennacherib! . . . and so much for Sennacherib's god!

Worse yet, Sennacherib was killed by his own people while he was worshipping his god Nisroch. (2 Kings 19:37) Neither Sennacherib, his god, nor his armies were a match for the power of the Lord God of Israel!

A little later, when Hezekiah was sick unto death, he prayed to the Lord: **"I beseech Thee, O LORD, remember now how I have walked before Thee in truth and with a perfect heart, and have done that which is good in Thy sight. And Hezekiah wept sore."** (2 Kings 20:3)

This shows the tender heart of Hezekiah towards the Lord. This was a man with whom the Lord God could (and did) have fellowship, even though Hezekiah was a descendant of Adam! Based on this prayer, the Lord granted Hezekiah 15 more years of life!

27

Manasseh Was As Evil
As Hezekiah Was Good!

There isn't much bad one can say about Hezekiah. He was a sinner, compliments of Adam, but as men go, Hezekiah was pretty good. Hezekiah walked with the Lord as much as we have seen any king since David. . . . and that meant the Lord could have fellowship with Hezekiah!

We do **not** know how Hezekiah's example carried over to his people. We **do** know, however, how his example carried over to his son. Hezekiah's son Manasseh totally rejected everything he saw his father do!

Hezekiah's Son Manasseh

When we consider Hezekiah's son, Manasseh, one wonders if the two men were even related. As good as Hezekiah was, and as much as he walked with the Lord, Manasseh was his total opposite!

What do we read about Manasseh?

"²And he did that which was evil in the sight of the LORD, after the abominations of the heathen, whom the LORD cast out before the children of Israel.

³For he built up again the high places which Hezekiah his father had destroyed; and he reared up altars for Baal, and made a grove, as did Ahab king of Israel; and worshipped all the host of heaven, and served them. ⁴And he built altars in the house of the LORD, of which the LORD said, 'In Jerusalem will I put My name.' ⁵And he built altars for all the host of heaven in the two courts of the house of the LORD. ⁶And

he made his son pass through the fire, and observed times, and used enchantments, and dealt with familiar spirits and wizards: he wrought much wickedness in the sight of the LORD, to provoke Him to anger.

^{7}And he set a graven image of the grove that he had made in the house, of which the LORD said to David, and to Solomon his son, 'In this house, and in Jerusalem, which I have chosen out of all tribes of Israel, will I put My name for ever.' " (2 Kings 21:2-7)

Manasseh was totally wicked! He set up all the heathen idols and gods, along with their paraphernalia, which his father had pulled down and destroyed! . . . and he went much, much further: he put idols and false gods into the house of the Lord which was totally forbidden!

The Temple was the Lord's house! Manasseh treated it as a house of worship to any and all gods. Simply put, he committed great abominations before the Lord! . . . and according to verses 5-6, every type of evil, every type of idolatry, and every type of dark, heathen practice was part of Manasseh's repertoire!

Although the people had received explicit instructions in the law from the Lord concerning how to behave, we read of the people in Manasseh's day, **"But they hearkened not: and Manasseh seduced them to do more evil than did the nations whom the LORD destroyed before the children of Israel."** (2 Kings 21:9)

Not only was Manasseh an evil, wicked king, but he led the children of Israel down that dark path with him! They were seduced by his wicked, abominable practices! . . . and they committed worse abominations than the people of the land of Canaan, whom Joshua and company were supposed to have destroyed or driven out!

In one generation, the tribe of Judah went from having one of the greatest kings ever, to having one of the worst!

The Lord's Response to Manasseh

What was the Lord's response to Manasseh?
"^{11}Because Manasseh king of Judah hath done these abominations, and hath done wickedly above all that the Amorites did, which were before him, and hath made Judah also to sin with his idols: ^{12}therefore thus saith the LORD God of Israel, 'Behold, I am bringing such evil upon Jerusalem and Judah, that whosoever heareth of it, both

his ears shall tingle. ¹³And I will stretch over Jerusalem the line of Samaria, and the plummet of the house of Ahab: and I will wipe Jerusalem as a man wipeth a dish, wiping it, and turning it upside down. ¹⁴And I will forsake the remnant of mine inheritance, and deliver them into the hand of their enemies; and they shall become a prey and a spoil to all their enemies; ¹⁵because they have done that which was evil in My sight, and have provoked Me to anger, since the day their fathers came forth out of Egypt, even unto this day." (2 Kings 21:11-15)

The Lord was angry with Manasseh, and with the people whom he seduced. His anger began to be kindled by the children of Israel whom He rescued from Egypt, and since that day, the people's behavior only grew worse and worse!

There was hardly any possibility for fellowship with anyone in Manasseh's day. Maybe there were some (one or two???) individuals with whom the Lord could fellowship, but the king, and his followers, provided no opportunities for fellowship whatsoever!

The people of Manasseh's day all demonstrated that they were born in Adam's image and likeness, and that they were terribly flawed! They wanted nothing to do with the Lord God of Israel, regardless how much He had done for them!

The people's behavior didn't improve after Manasseh died, because the next king, his son Amon, took after his father. "²¹And he walked in all the way that his father walked in, and served the idols that his father served, and worshipped them. ²²And he forsook the LORD God of his fathers, and walked not in the way of the LORD." (2 Kings 21:21-22)

Amon's own servants "conspired against him" and put him to death! (2 Kings 21:23) . . . and his people were so loyal to him and his evil ways, that they killed all those who participated in his demise!

The Lord would have to wait to have a people of His own who would truly love Him, obey Him, and want to fellowship with Him!

Yet amazingly enough, the Lord was still open to the people's call for help! He was still ready to help if and when they called to Him!

The Lord demonstrated during the days of Manasseh and Amon that He is an extremely patient and longsuffering God! . . . and He showed His extreme patience over and over again to the children of Israel throughout Old Testament times.

Josiah Was An Even Better King Than Hezekiah

We just said there was little opportunity for God to fellowship with anyone during the reigns of Manasseh and Amon. . . . but there had to be some men and women of God in the land as the next king, Josiah, demonstrated!

After a whole series of good kings, we saw that king Hezekiah was a really great king! He was unlike any we had seen before him except for maybe king David!

Then, there came his son Manasseh, who was truly evil and wicked in all his ways! Manasseh's son Amon took after his father. The apple didn't fall far from the tree in Amon's case.

But then came Josiah, Amon's son. Josiah was in the league of good kings with Hezekiah and David! He might have been even better than Hezekiah, if that's possible! It's truly amazing, but that's the way it goes with fallen mankind!

In those days, the pendulum of behavior towards the Lord was swinging wildly back and forth — from extremely good to extremely evil.

Josiah, King of Judah

Josiah was 8 years old when he became king of Judah, and he reigned for 31 years. We do not know from whom he learned of the Lord God of Israel, but he did learn of Him! . . . and he was faithful to Him!

"And he did that which was right in the sight of the LORD, and walked in all the way of David his father, and turned not aside to the right hand or to the left." (2 Kings 22:2)

Josiah walked the straight and narrow path which king David walked with the Lord. He didn't allow any distractions to send him off on any tangents.

After the reigns of Manasseh and Amon, the house of the Lord needed cleaning out and fixing. Josiah put money directly into the hands of the builders who were assigned to repair the structure. Verse 7 says that he made no reckoning with the builders, which means the priests gave the money directly to the builders and the builders were answerable to the Lord to make the repairs. That is a wonderful way to fix the house of the Lord! No micro-managing there!

The Book of the Law

The high priest at that time, Hilkiah, **"found the book of the law in the house of the LORD."** (2 Kings 22:8) Where else would one expect to keep a book like that? . . . and yet they **FOUND** it in the house of the Lord! . . . as if it was lost!

Actually, that's exactly what had happened. **The book of the law had been lost!** . . . and it hadn't been consulted for years! Someone put it in an out of the way place in the Temple where it collected dust for years, out of sight, out of mind!

But Hilkiah found it and showed it to Shaphan, Josiah's scribe. Shaphan read it and brought it to Josiah, who ordered it read to him. Then, realizing that the people were all guilty of all manner of sins before the Lord, Josiah **"rent his clothes."** He realized that the wrath of the Lord would be **"great"** against the children of Israel because they had been ignoring the Lord's commands!

Josiah commanded his servants, **"Go ye, enquire of the LORD for me, and for the people, and for all Judah, concerning the words of this book that is found: for great is the wrath of the LORD that is kindled against us, because our fathers have not hearkened unto the words of this book, to do according unto all that which is written concerning us."** (2 Kings 22:13)

Then, Josiah gathered all the people — everyone — and "**he read in their ears all the words of the book of the covenant which was found in the house of the LORD.**" (2 Kings 23:2)

This was a good move on Josiah's part. The people should have been hearing the words of the book of the law all throughout those years when the book had been ignored. One wonders how often the people had heard the words of the law? . . . or if they had ever heard them?

It appears that for many years, the children of Israel did not hear the words of the law, and they had no idea what the law actually said! Does this sound familiar? Does anyone today really know what's contained in the Bible? It's the world's best-selling book! . . . and probably also, the world's least-read book!

Josiah realized there was a major problem at hand, and he attempted to remedy the situation as best he could!

House Cleaning

Notice: vessels for Baal had been placed in the Temple of the Lord. Vessels for the groves, and for all the host of heaven, were sitting in the house of the Lord! Some of the priests, "**idolatrous priests,**" burned incense in high places. Other priests burned incense "**unto Baal, to the sun, and to the moon, and to the planets, and to all the host of heaven.**" (2 Kings 23:5) Josiah "**put down**" all these priests! He stopped them from continuing their heathen practices! This could even mean that he put them to death!

Josiah brought the heathen idols out of the house of the Lord and burned them! (vs 6) He "**brake down the houses of the sodomites**" who served by the house of the Lord. (vs 8) He "**brake down the high places of the gates.**" All of these high places were served by priests of the people (apparently Levitical priests). The verses which describe Josiah's cleanup go on and on.

Then, after the cleanup, he commanded the people, once again, to keep the Passover. It hadn't been mentioned in a long time! Those of us today reading the Old Testament might assume that the people were observing the Passover annually throughout all those years, but apparently, they were not observing it at all! Josiah ordered the people to begin to observe it once again!

Josiah also "**put away**" all those who worked with "**familiar spirits,**" as well as "**the wizards, and the images, and the idols, and all the abominations that were spied in the land of Judah and in Jerusalem.**" (2 Kings 23:24)

Josiah accomplished a major cleaning of the house of the Lord by removing all of the evil, heathen vessels and practices which had entered therein.

Josiah's Relationship with the Lord

"**And like unto him was there no king before him, that turned to the LORD with all his heart, and with all his soul, and with all his might, according to all the law of Moses; neither after him arose there any like him.**" (2 Kings 23:25)

We don't read anything like this of any of the kings before Josiah! This is unique commentary for a king of Judah! There were none like Josiah in this regard — who "**turned to the LORD with all his heart, and with all his soul, and with all his might**"!

Yet even this was not enough to assuage the Lord's anger! He promised to send the people of Judah and Jerusalem into captivity in far away lands. The Lord was going to remove them from the land of promise and send them to places out of His sight!

Even though we see here a good king who totally served the Lord, it was not enough to turn the Lord's anger away from the people.

The people demonstrated again that indwelling sin was taking over their hearts and minds; they wanted nothing to do with the Lord; and despite Josiah's efforts, the Lord's anger remained kindled against them!

Personally, Josiah wanted to serve the Lord! He also wanted the people to serve the Lord. It appears that the Lord credited Josiah with this desire to serve Him, but the Lord found similar desire lacking among the people. Some may have followed Josiah's lead, but many did not!

29

Josiah's Sons Jehoahaz & Jehoiakim Sinned

King Josiah did his best to fix the relationship between the people of Israel and the Lord, but he was unsuccessful. The Lord surely appreciated Josiah's efforts, and his own relationship with the Lord was pretty good. But the Lord knew the hearts of the people! ... and Josiah's efforts among the people, which were mostly cosmetic, did not touch the hearts of many of the people.

When Josiah died, three of his sons reigned, and they reverted back to following in the line of the evil kings of Judah! The pendulum had swung to the opposite extreme once again! One would think the sons of Josiah might have taken after their father, or after Hezekiah, but they did not. They took after earlier evil kings, like Manasseh.

Jehoahaz

King Josiah was killed in battle by Pharaohnechoh, king of Egypt. When Josiah died, the people of Judah anointed Josiah's younger son, 23 year old Jehoahaz, as the new king.

Jehoahaz reigned for only 3 months in Jerusalem. What did he do during that time? **"And he did that which was evil in the sight of the LORD, according to all that his fathers had done."** (2 Kings 23:32)

Jehoahaz' reign was cut short because Pharaohnechoh took him prisoner and carried him off to Egypt.

Jehoiakim

Pharaohnechoh installed 25 year old Eliakim, elder son of Josiah, as the new king of Judah. Then, pharaoh changed Eliakim's name to Jehoiakim. *Eliakim* means "God will raise up," *Jehoiakim* means "Jehovah will raise up." (Newberry Bible, margin, 2 Kings 23:34)

It appears pharaoh changed Eliakim's name — just because he could. When a king changed a name, the action showed that he considered himself to be in charge! Actually, as we know, the Lord was in charge! . . . but pharaoh didn't know nor believe that.

Jehoiakim reigned for 11 years in Jerusalem. How did Jehoiakim behave towards the Lord?

"And he did that which was evil in the sight of the LORD, according to all that his fathers had done." (2 Kings 23:37)

At first, Jehoiakim had to deal with Pharaohnechoh. Then, he became the servant of Nebuchadnezzar, king of Babylon. (2 Kings 24:1)

The Lord sent several armies against Judah. Jehoiakim had to deal with the armies of the Egyptians, the Babylonians, the Chaldeans, the Syrians, the Moabites, and the Ammonites. The goal of these armies was to destroy Judah. (2 Kings 24:2) The author of 2 Kings said the Lord wanted to destroy Judah because of **"the sins of Manasseh."** (2 Kings 24:3) Manasseh had **"filled Jerusalem with innocent blood; which the LORD would not pardon."** (2 Kings 24:4)

The Lord was following through with His promise to send the people into captivity to their enemies in foreign lands!

Summary

Josiah was a really good king, but his two sons were the exact opposite! They did only evil in the eyes of the Lord!

The Lord's anger had been sufficiently kindled that He was going to punish the children of Israel by sending them off into captivity in foreign lands. The people didn't want to serve the Lord! . . . so He was showing them what it would be like to be slaves of foreign kings in far-away lands.

After Jehoiakim, only two more kings of Judah reigned before Nebuchadnezzar took the people of Judah into captivity in Babylon:

Jehoiakim's son, Jehoiachin, and Jehoiakim's brother Mattaniah (who was renamed Zedekiah.) King Zedekiah was in power when the children of Judah were taken captive to Babylon. Both of these last two kings also did evil before the Lord!

So the people were carried off to Babylon where they were in captivity for seventy years. The Lord orchestrated the captivities of Israel in Assyria, and Judah in Babylon, in payment for their rejection of Him!

The Lord's ability to fellowship with a people of His own was mostly put on hold. He hadn't changed His goals, but His dealings with the children of Israel were just not working. All the children of Israel were born in the image and likeness of Adam, and their behavior had deteriorated so it was on a par with the behavior of natural man before the flood.

A new beginning was soon to occur. This time, however, the beginning was going to take a different form. The Lord was about to send His own beloved Son to earth to be born as a man. The Lord Jesus would make possible a new generation of children of God on earth.

The Lord had given every opportunity to the children of Israel to be His people and to worship Him, but mostly, they were not interested. All through the Old Testament, the Lord worked with the children of the patriarchs, but they rejected Him!

Do not think this new beginning was a last minute idea by the Lord to salvage mankind for the Lord. This solution was planned by the Father and the Son before the foundations of the world. The fulness of time had come to send Jesus to earth.

We certainly know that the Lord had great and wonderful fellowship with His Son throughout eternity past and throughout Old Testament times. That fellowship would continue when Jesus walked this earth as a man.

Jesus' generation of children of God is the generation of believers who will truly worship and love God. . . . and this generation will be the one with whom God, and His Son Jesus Christ, will spend eternity!

New Testament believers are men, women, and children who love the Lord, who appreciate all He has done for them, who rejoice at the opportunity to spend eternity in His presence, who completely appreciate the Lord God and His Son Jesus Christ, and who will enjoy every minute of eternity in God the Father's and God the Son's presences!

30

A Final New Start
with Jesus Christ, Son of God

About 500 years after the captivity of the Jewish people in Babylon, the Lord God sent His Son to earth to walk among us as a man. During the years between the captivity and the birth of Jesus, there was still the possibility for the Lord to fellowship with children of Israel, such as demonstrated by Daniel, Hananiah, Mishael, and Azariah. (Daniel 1:6)

But fellowship opportunities in those years were few. The Jewish people had almost completely abandoned the Lord, and the time was right for Him to make big changes.

In the book of Malachi, last book of the Old Testament, the Lord charged the children of Israel with rejecting His overtures, despising Him, profaning His holiness, wearying Him, rejecting His ordinances, robbing Him, and speaking out against Him! The response of the people to all of those accusations was essentially, "Who??? Us??? We didn't do that! Noooooo!!" The Lord had finally had it with the Jewish people! Enough was enough!

So following Malachi, we saw God take a totally different approach. He sent His Son to live among us where He could be God's communication to mankind!

The House of David

King David wanted to build a permanent house for the Lord in Jerusalem, but the Lord would not allow him to do so. The Lord told

David that as a man of war, he would **not** build the Lord a house. But David's son Solomon, who was a man of peace, would build the Lord a house.

At that same time, however, the Lord told David, "**and thine house and thy kingdom shall be established for ever before thee: thy throne shall be established for ever.**" (2 Samuel 7:16)

David wanted to build a **physical** house for the Lord. Instead, the Lord said **He** was going to build David a house. David's house which the Lord promised to build would be a spiritual house! . . . and it would be "**established for ever.**" The descriptor "**for ever**" doesn't apply to physical houses — but it does apply to spiritual houses! . . . and that is the big change that begins in the New Testament! In fact, David is mentioned in the very first verse of the New Testament!

Jesus Christ, Son of David

The New Testament begins with these words: "**The book of the generation of Jesus Christ, the son of David, the son of Abraham.**" (Matthew 1:1)

Jesus Christ is the representative of the godhead (the "**Prophet**") God promised to send among the children of Israel. Through Moses, the Lord sent this message to the people:

"**15The LORD thy God will raise up unto thee <u>a Prophet</u> from the midst of thee, of thy brethren, like unto me; unto Him ye shall hearken; 16according to all that thou desiredst of the LORD thy God in Horeb in the day of the assembly, saying, 'Let me not hear again the voice of the LORD my God, neither let me see this great fire any more, that I die not.' **" (Deuteronomy 18:15-16)

The people were afraid when the Lord God spoke within their hearing on mount Sinai because His booming voice was accompanied by dark clouds, thunder, and lightning! . . . and to prevent the people's fear, the Lord promised to send a Prophet among them who would be one of them! This promised prophet, a human, would speak God's words directly to them! They would no longer need to fear when God spoke!

Moses said this Prophet would be "**like unto me.**" (vs 15) From history, we know that this Prophet was Jesus Christ, Son of God!

Jesus would speak the Lord's words directly to the people! He was the Lord God, Creator of the universe, whose words Moses gave to the people throughout the Pentateuch! He was not only the Son of God, He was the very message sent by God to mankind; He was the heir of all things; He was the Creator of the worlds; He was the brightness of God's glory; He was the express image of God's Person; He was the Maintainer of all things; and He was the Savior of the world!

Here is the passage:

"¹**God, who at sundry times and in divers manners spake in time past unto the fathers by the prophets, ²hath in these last days spoken unto us by His Son, whom He hath appointed heir of all things, by whom also He made the worlds;**

³**Who being the brightness of His glory, and the express image of His person, and upholding all things by the word of His power, when He had by Himself purged our sins, sat down on the right hand of the Majesty on high.**" (Hebrews 1:1-3)

A rubber stamp and the image it makes are "**express**" images of each other. (vs 3) Each one is fully representative of the other! The Son of God, by whom God spoke in these last days (vs 2), was "**the express image**" of the Father. "**No man hath seen God at any time.**" (1 John 4:12) Not even Moses saw God when He passed by Moses on the mountain, but all who have seen Jesus, the Son, know perfectly what the Father is like because Jesus Christ is the express image of God the Father!

Jesus was God's message to the people! (Hebrews 1:2) God spoke to man "**in Son.**" Jesus was the messenger! Jesus was the message!

This is Jesus Christ, Son of God, son of David, the new covenant in God's relationship with mankind!

Jesus Came Unto His Own!

Moses told the children of Israel that God would send "**a Prophet**" unto them. (Deuteronomy 18:15)

God sent Jesus unto the Jewish people! In the New Testament, the Apostle John wrote that Jesus Christ, "**came unto His own, and His own received Him not.**" (John 1:11)

Who were "**His own**"? The Jewish people were "**His own**"! Jesus was born unto Mary and her espoused husband Joseph, both of whom were descendants of king David. Jesus was born into a Jewish family! . . . and the Jews were the ones who rejected Him!

Let's be clear: God was Jesus' father, Mary was His human mother. This is explained in Isaiah 9:6:

> "For unto us <u>a child is born</u>,
> Unto us <u>a son is given</u>:
> And the government shall be upon His shoulder:
> And His name shall be called Wonderful, Counsellor,
> The Mighty God, The Everlasting Father, The Prince of Peace."

The Holy Spirit was very clear with His choice of words in this passage: Jesus Christ, the baby in the manger in Bethlehem, was **the child** who was "**born**." Mary carried him for 9 months in a normal pregnancy. Jesus was fully human!

But Jesus is also **the Son** who was "**given**." The Son of God wasn't born that day — the Son of God, who was alive for all eternity, was "**given**"! God the Father **gave** His Son to mankind! The Son was the person who was known to the people throughout the Old Testament as "**the LORD.**" Jesus, the eternal Son of God, became a man.

"¹In the beginning was the Word, and the Word was with God, and the Word was God. ²The same was in the beginning with God." (John 1:1-2)

The man we know as Jesus Christ ever existed as the Son of God! He existed "**in the beginning.**" This expression in John 1:1, takes us well before Genesis 1:1, into eternity past!

Jesus Christ, Son of God, was the Prophet of the house of David, whom God sent among the people to present His Word to them! . . . and that is exactly what Jesus did while He was here!

"Now I say that Jesus Christ was a minister of the circumcision for the truth of God, <u>to confirm the promises</u> made unto the fathers." (Romans 15:8)

This was Paul's explanation — Jesus came unto the Jews (to "**the circumcision**") "**to confirm the promises made unto the fathers.**" Jesus came among mankind to speak **for** God! . . . to speak **as** God!

"...and His Own Received Him Not"!

This heading is the second half of John 1:11. Jesus' own, which included all Jews, rejected Him! They rejected God's rule over them in the Old Testament when they insisted God give them a king! Then, they rejected the King when He came to live among them!

"And ye have this day rejected your God, who Himself saved you out of all your adversities and your tribulations; and ye have said unto Him, 'Nay, but set a king over us.' " (1 Samuel 10:19)

In the New Testament, they rejected the King when God sent Him to earth to live among His people. Jesus told the people a parable about Himself! In it, they rejected Him! Jesus knew the heart of the people very well!

"But his citizens hated him, and sent a message after him, saying, 'We will not have this man to reign over us.' " (Luke 19:14)

The Jewish people of Jesus' day demonstrated this statement to be absolutely true when they called for (Luke 23:21), and carried out (Luke 23:33) Jesus' crucifixion!

At Jesus' trial, Pilate asked the people if he should crucify their King. They denied He was their King: **"But they cried out, 'Away with Him, away with Him, crucify Him.' Pilate saith unto them, 'Shall I crucify your King?' The chief priests answered, 'We have no king but Caesar.' "** (John 19:15)

Pilate recognized that Jesus was their King! ...and he ordered this sign to be placed on Jesus' cross: **"THIS IS JESUS THE KING OF THE JEWS."** (Matthew 27:37)

Jesus came unto His own people — the Jewish people — and they received Him not!

Faith Is the Key!

"For God so loved the world, that He gave His only begotten Son, that whosoever <u>believeth</u> in Him should not perish, but have everlasting life." (John 3:16)

The Greek word *pistis* is translated *faith, belief.* The verb *pisteuō* is translated *to believe. Faith* is a noun with no verb form. *Belief* is also a noun with its verb form *to believe.* So when we see forms of the verb **to believe**, it means *to have faith — to have belief.*

Whosoever <u>believes</u> — that is, whosoever <u>puts their faith in</u> the Lord Jesus Christ will not perish, but have everlasting life. What must we believe? In whom must we place our faith? We must believe that the Son of God, Jesus Christ, died on the cross with the full burden of our sins, and the sins of the whole world, heaped upon His shoulders.

All we need to do is to look to Jesus' work on Calvary in faith, believe in Him, and we will not perish, but have everlasting life! Can it be that simple? Yes! It can!

We know that **"the wages of sin is death."** (Romans 6:23) Adam sinned and he died! He died spiritually instantly! . . . and he died physically at the end of his long life. Then, he was buried! He sinned, and he died — spiritually and physically!

That happens to each and every one of us! Having been born in Adam's image and likeness, we no longer bear the image or likeness of God because Adam lost them both! . . . and as sinners (also compliments of Adam) our spirits are already dead to God. At the end of our lives, we all face physical death! . . . and after we die physically, we will all stand before God and face the consequences of our sins!

All those sinners who have rejected God, will face eternity in the blackness of darkness of hell! Sin, and the rejection of God without putting any faith in Him, brings punishment for our own sins upon us!

The beauty of God's solution is that Jesus Christ, who committed no sins of His own, took all punishments upon Himself which we (all of us) deserve!

Jesus was forsaken by God while He hanged on the cross under the burden of our sins! He took our punishment upon Himself, but since He did not commit any sins of His own, death had no claim on Him!

Death could not hold Jesus because He committed no sins! . . . but He paid all penalties before God for all of **our** sins!

The Righteous God, who cannot ignore sin, has not ignored it! The required punishments for all sins of mankind were paid-in-full by Jesus Christ while He hanged on the cross!

At the judgment, when God asks each believer, "What do you have to say for yourself?" believers can say, "I am a sinner! . . . but my Lord Jesus Christ paid all penalties for my sins!" When God looks over to

Jesus, He will say, "Yes! This brother/sister is one of mine!" God can then respond favorably toward us because the punishment for our sins has been paid-in-full! . . . by Jesus Christ! God's righteous requirement of punishment for sins committed has been satisfied! . . . and God can say to each believer, "Welcome, beloved!"

When non-believers, which includes all those who rejected God in this lifetime, who tried to live perfect lives apart from God, and who wanted nothing to do with Jesus Christ, stand before God at the judgment, they will be found "Guilty!" Each of them will then be sentenced to pay all punishments due for their own sins!

That's not a pretty thought! . . . and it's a great waste! . . . because Jesus already paid all penalties for their sins! . . . but if they refuse His offer . . . they will pay for their own sins!

The Burden On Jesus Was Enormous!

The magnitude of the burden necessary to pay for all sins of all men, women, and children of all times, was just enormous! It cannot be quantified!

God's desire is that all men be saved! All!

"The Lord is not slack concerning His promise, as some men count slackness; but is longsuffering to us-ward, not willing that any should perish, but that all should come to repentance." (2 Peter 3:9)

Some teach that God chooses who will be His, and who won't be His. That teaching is only partially correct. Yes, God chooses who will be His! . . . and He chooses **all** of us! He chooses **everyone!**

The Lord doesn't want any of us to perish! He wants **all** to come to repentance. ALL!! . . . and in order for that to be possible, Jesus paid all penalties for all sins ever committed when He died for all mankind! That suffering was an enormous, immeasurable burden!

"But we see Jesus, who was made a little lower than the angels for the suffering of death, crowned with glory and honour; that He by the grace of God should taste death for <u>every</u> man." (Hebrews 2:9)

Notice that this verse doesn't end with ". . . that He should taste death for <u>some</u> men." Neither does it say, ". . . that He should taste death for <u>a few</u> men." It says, "**. . . that He should taste death for <u>every</u> man."**

So when God chose those who will be His, He chose **all**! . . . **everyone**! . . . **every man**! Those who are not the Lord's people are not — because **they** rejected the Lord!

How can God say He wants "<u>all</u>" to come to repentance if He was only going to choose some? Why should Jesus "**taste death for <u>every</u> man**" if God was only going to choose to save some?

Neither God, nor Jesus, misunderstood the magnitude of the problem. They knew! "**For all have sinned and come short of the glory of God.**" (Romans 3:23) They knew! . . . and Jesus gave His life anyway!

Free Will

God knew when He created man that to make us like Him meant He had to give us free will. . . . and God knew that to give man free will would mean He would have to deal with sin and death. God knew that the solution to sin and death was to send His Son, Jesus Christ, to walk this earth and die on the cross under the load of **our** sins. God knew! Jesus knew!

Jesus came knowing exactly what He would face! In Hebrews 10:7,9, the writer twice quoted Jesus' words: "**Lo, I come to do thy will, O God.**" Jesus knew the cost! . . . and He came anyway! Jesus loves mankind more than any of us can know! . . . and He came to save us! Jesus knew the vile treatment He would face at the hands of man! . . . and He came anyway! Jesus knew the punishment for our sins He would face at God's hands! . . . and He came anyway!

So God made us all like Him — with free will! Adam chose to disobey God! Adam rejected God! The children of Israel disobeyed God! The children of Israel rejected God! . . . and we have that same choice today: to obey or **not** to obey! . . . and to believe or to reject God!

Since Adam already rejected the Lord, and we were all born in Adam's image and likeness, we don't need to reject the Lord. We are all born separated from the Lord, compliments of Adam! Our spirits are dead to God, compliments of Adam! If we do nothing, we have already rejected Him!

But we can all accept Him! . . . and that is what God would like every one of us to do! . . . every man, woman, and child! . . . and that would make God most happy!

Many, however, will not accept God's offer because it just sounds too easy! The point they miss is that if God hadn't made it totally easy, no one would ever enter God's presence!

Eternal life is a gift of God! (Romans 6:23) It is not something we can work for and achieve! All we need to do is **accept** His gift! All we need to do is **believe** Him!

31

Jesus Did No Sin

The New Testament introduces and describes the life of Jesus Christ, the Son of God. In the Old Testament, the Lord wanted everyone to love, obey, and worship Him with all their hearts, minds, and souls. That is still the case in the New Testament!

In the Old Testament, the first man Adam disobeyed the Lord, and his fallen nature was passed along to every one of his descendants!

In the years after that event, the Lord was very patient and longsuffering toward the children of Israel, and toward strangers who wanted to walk with the Lord. But as more and more children of Israel rejected Him, the Lord's wrath increased until He sent all of them into captivity in foreign lands.

When the people tired of their subservience to foreign kings, they called for the Lord to rescue them — and He did!

In the New Testament, God sent the Lord to live among mankind in the person of His Son, Jesus Christ. God sent Jesus to rescue mankind from slavery to sin — and He did!

The man Jesus, the Son of God, was born a child to Mary. Jesus did not reject nor disobey God throughout His whole life! He did not have a fallen nature like His brethren because His Father was God, not Adam!

The solution to mankind's sin problem is to put one's faith in the Person, works, and words of Jesus Christ. Today, we see many men, women, and children who were once walking totally separated from God, turning to, and calling upon the Lord to rescue them and bring them into His fold.

Once men, women, and children realize they have reached rock bottom, and they don't like their prospects at the bottom of the pit, they can call upon the Lord in a humble attitude of faith. . . . and He will lift them out of the pit and empower them, so they can actually begin to do good works pleasing to the Lord! They can also then begin to fellowship with the Father.

To Sin vs Sinners

Here is an important question: Are we sinners because we commit sins? . . . or . . . Do we commit sins because we are sinners? This is a "chicken or egg" question! Which comes first?

Many people believe they are sinners because they have committed sins. In that case, if they can just stop sinning, they will no longer be sinners. Right? . . . Wrong! Wrong answer!

The problem is that we have each inherited the sin nature from our ancestor Adam, so **we are sinners!** . . . and **because we are sinners, we commit sins!** This means that if we could somehow stop ourselves from committing sins, we would still, nevertheless, be sinners!

That is the correct answer to the question: **We are sinners! Therefore we commit sins!**

All mankind have this problem. We have all been born in the image and likeness of our ancestor Adam! We **are** sinners! . . . and for that reason, we commit sins!

If we managed somehow to stop sinning, we remain sinners! If we managed somehow to live perfect lives, we remain sinners! . . . and as sinners, what can **we** do? Nothing! That is the problem all mankind faces! That is the problem Jesus Christ addressed! That is the problem Jesus Christ solved! We cannot solve the sin problem, but Jesus can, and did, solve it for us!

Jesus' Father Was Not Adam

Jesus is different from all the rest of us because His Father was not Adam! Jesus' Father is God! His mother was Mary, but His Father is God! . . . and this takes us back to that verse, Isaiah 9:6, which says "**unto us a child is born,**" but "**unto us a son is given**"!

God **gave** His eternal Son to become a man by being **born** into this world to Mary. Jesus' conception was the work of the Holy Spirit! (Matthew 1:20)

It was a miracle of God for the Son to be born as a human. The writer of Hebrews said that the Son of God was made like us so He could know all facets of this life and serve us well! Jesus was fully man, but also fully God! . . . and since Jesus' father is God, not Adam, He was born **without** indwelling sin!

"**¹⁶For verily He took not on Him the nature of angels; but He took on Him the seed of Abraham. ¹⁷Wherefore in all things it behoved Him to be made like unto His brethren, that He might be a merciful and faithful high priest in things pertaining to God, to make reconciliation for the sins of the people. ¹⁸For in that He Himself hath suffered being tempted, He is able to succour them that are tempted.**" (Hebrews 2:16-18)

Jesus took the form of a man so He could experience life as a man. He was tempted in this world as we are, yet without sin. There was no sin in Him to respond to the temptations of this life.

When one dangles a carrot in front of the nose of a donkey, it will usually move forward toward the carrot. The carrot is the temptation — but the carrot alone is not sin. Being exposed to the carrot is being exposed to a temptation. The temptation alone is not sin. What a person does with the temptation, however — **that** may or may not be a sin. When we are tempted, how we respond determines whether or not we sin.

To say that Jesus was tempted, means that all manner of carrots were dangled in front of Him. . . . but there was no sin in Him to cause Him to respond to any of those temptations! There were no sinful desires in Jesus' heart to cause Him to respond to any of them! Similar temptations to those Jesus faced, however, would draw out sinful desires from our hearts which would overwhelm us!

There are three types of temptations all mankind must face: "**For all that is in the world, <u>the lust of the flesh</u>, and <u>the lust of the eyes</u>, and <u>the pride of life</u>, is not of the Father, but is of the world.**" (1 John 2:16)

These are the three types of temptations everyone faces: (1) the lust of the flesh, (2) the lust of the eyes, and (3) the pride of life. As John stated, all of these are "**of the world.**" Jesus had no sin nature in Him, so He did not respond to any of these temptations!

When Jesus was tempted in the wilderness, the devil used these three types of temptations to entice Him. . . . and Jesus did not succumb to any of the devil's enticements!

Jesus was **not** motivated by the flesh, by His eyes, nor by His pride. Being free from sin has great advantages! Jesus was motivated by His Father's will! Whatever the Father wanted Him to do, that He did!

There are several verses in the New Testament which teach us that Jesus was completely separate from sin! Let's consider them:

In Him Is No Sin

Jesus became a man so He could "**take away our sins.**" He could do that because "**in Him is no sin.**"

"**And ye know that He was manifested to take away our sins; and in Him is no sin.**" (1 John 3:5)

No other man was ever born like Jesus, Son of God. The Son existed forever — from eternity past! . . . but He became a man! Speaking of the man, Christ Jesus, Paul wrote:

"[5]**Let this mind be in you, which was also in Christ Jesus:** [6]**Who, being in the form of God, thought it not robbery to be equal with God:** [7]**but made Himself of no reputation, and took upon Him the form of a servant, and was made in the likeness of men:** [8]**and being found in fashion as a man, He humbled Himself, and became obedient unto death, even the death of the cross.**" (Philippians 2:5-8)

The Son of God was equal with God, but that was not something He clung to at all costs! Jesus was God! Had Jesus considered that fact to be of ultimate importance, He would never have become a man.

We have seen dictators in this world who, having once grasped power, would never ever consider giving up that power to take a lower place in society! They cling to that power! . . . but Jesus does not think like that! Inherently, He is much greater than any dictator — He is God! . . . and yet He came to earth as a child of Mary!

He made Himself of no reputation; He was born as a baby; He took the form of a servant; and He was made in the likeness of men. As an adult in "**fashion as a man,**" He humbled Himself, obeyed His Father's every wish, and sacrificed His life on the cross for sinful man!

Jesus lived for 33½ years on earth as a man, yet in Him was no sin! Death had no claim on Him! Had He not voluntarily given up His life at the end of the crucifixion, He would not have died. It was impossible that any man could kill Him! No one on earth had the power to take Jesus' life from Him! No one on earth had the power to take God's life from Him! Jesus gave up the ghost freely and willingly at the end of the crucifixion!

As men go, Jesus was unique! Being **"in the form of God,"** He was made **"in the likeness of men."** . . . and even though He was **"in fashion as a man,"** He was without sin! **"In Him is no sin"**!

The word *form* means "*shape*; figuratively *nature*." (Strong's) The word *likeness* means "a *form*; abstractly *resemblance*." (Strong's) The word *fashion* means "a *figure* (as a mode or circumstance), that is (by implication) external *condition*." (Strong's)

Inherently, Jesus was God; His form and fashion were as a man; and He was without sin! He gave His life for us! He suffered under the load of **our** sins! He died taking the place of punishment each of **us** deserves! He died for **"every man."** (Hebrews 2:9)

He Knew No Sin

Not only was there no sin in Him, but He **"knew no sin"**! There was nothing in Him which was the least bit familiar with sin! . . . and yet, He became sin for us! Why? . . . that we might be righteous!

"For He hath made Him to be sin for us, <u>who knew no sin</u>; that we might be made the righteousness of God in Him." (2 Corinthians 5:21)

Rearranging the first part of this verse makes it more clear: **"For He hath made Him,"** **"who knew no sin,"** **"to be sin for us."**

Jesus died in **our** place that we might stand righteous before God! Apart from being made righteous by the Lord God, we — mankind — would **never** be righteous!

The word *righteous* means "*equitable* (in character or act); by implication *innocent, holy* (absolutely or relatively)." (Strong's)

Apart from God making mankind *holy*, there is no way any of us who are descendants of fallen Adam would ever be *holy*! Through Jesus' righteousness, we can be righteous when we stand before God!

He Is Without Sin

There was no sin in Him and He knew no sin. As one would therefore expect, Jesus was totally **without sin**! As a man, Jesus was a high priest — the Great High Priest — and He was untouched by sin! He was tempted in all points like the rest of us. The enticements of the eye, of the flesh, and of pride were all present — dangled before Him. But there was nothing in Him to respond to those enticements! He was without sin! He had no sin nature! He was perfectly pure throughout His whole life!

"For we have not an high priest which cannot be touched with the feeling of our infirmities; but was in all points tempted like as we are, yet without sin." (Hebrews 4:15)

He did everything in obedience to the Father! He pleased the Father constantly! That was His driving motivation! We know this because the Father expressed His delight in the Son on two different occasions. God said, **"This is My beloved Son, in whom I am well pleased"**! (Matthew 3:17, 17:5)

He Did No Sin

Jesus behaved like Adam was supposed to behave! Adam disobeyed God! Jesus was ever faithful and obedient to God, His Father, in all things. Adam should have been obedient, too, but he chose not to be. To demonstrate how a true child of God behaves, Jesus set the example for all to see!

"[21]For even hereunto were ye called: because Christ also suffered for us, leaving us an example, that ye should follow His steps: [22]Who did no sin, neither was guile found in His mouth: [23]Who, when He was reviled, reviled not again; when He suffered, He threatened not; but committed Himself to Him that judgeth righteously: [24]Who His own self bare our sins in His own body on the tree, that we, being dead to sins, should live unto righteousness: by whose stripes ye were healed." (1 Peter 2:21-24)

Jesus set a wonderful example for all of us. He did no sin and He did not commit any verbal sins. When someone treated Him poorly and unjustly, He took it in silence. When He suffered because of poor treatment, He did not retaliate nor threaten in return. He committed Himself unto God the Judge! Everything He did was to please God! . . .

and finally, He bore our sins on the cross, suffering at the hands of God under the load of **our** sins!

Why did He do this? . . . that we might become righteous! . . . that we might be healed by His stripes! . . . that we might live!

Sin had absolutely no part in Jesus being. . . . and He lives on, today, through eternity! There was never any question of that! Jesus took our sins upon Himself, and suffered for them, that we might live with Him! He knew exactly what He was doing!

Faith in Him

When a man, woman, or child believes and puts their faith in the Lord Jesus Christ, they accept His terrible death on the cross in payment to God for their own sins. Jesus died under the load of our sins! Before God, He suffered all punishments for those sins so we need not suffer the punishments ourselves!

Without our sins being paid in advance by Jesus Christ, our punishments would include permanent (eternal) banishment from the presence of God.

To suffer such punishments for **all** mankind is an enormous burden that Jesus took upon Himself! It is so enormous that we cannot even fathom its magnitude.

Jesus Christ suffered at the hands of God, on the cross, in unnatural darkness, for three hours from noon to 3 PM. It should have been the brightest part of the day, but it was not. God's back was turned! During that time, Jesus was forsaken by God. We know this because He told us! At the end of His ordeal, He cried out from the cross unto God: **"My God, My God, why hast Thou forsaken Me?"** (Matthew 27:46)

Three hours is a relatively short time in this world by mankind's reckoning. We do not know if there even is such a thing as time in heaven! Probably not! So those three hours of our time were an eternity to Jesus Christ and to God!

We know He suffered terribly during that time, but we cannot really appreciate the full extent of His sufferings! Our finite bodies, our limited minds, and our inferior understandings are insufficient to completely appreciate all that Jesus suffered for us during those three hours. The best we can say is that to fully understand His sufferings is beyond our ability to comprehend!

Those who put their faith in the Lord will have all eternity to learn the full extent of what He did for us while He suffered on the cross! . . . and we will need all eternity to really appreciate the full extent of the grace He showed each of us that day!

The Example Was Set

God wanted a people of His own here on earth with whom He could fellowship, love, care, spend time, etc. Adam failed to obey God; he sinned! . . . and after Adam sinned, he passed that sin nature on to each and every one of us!

But after four millennia, God sent His very Son, Jesus Christ, to live here among us and fulfill all that Adam should have fulfilled but did not.

Paul described it this way:

"**45And so it is written,**

The first man Adam was made a living soul;

> **The last Adam was made a quickening spirit.**

46Howbeit that was not first which is spiritual,

> **But that which is natural;**

And afterward that which is spiritual.

47The first man is of the earth, earthy;

> **The second man is the Lord from heaven.**"

(1 Corinthians 15:45-47)

Note that Paul mentions two Adams. Each Adam was the head of a family of men. The Adam whom God created in Genesis 1-2 was "**a living soul**" (vs 45); he is the one who is "**natural**" (vs 46); he is the one who sinned; and he is the one who is "**earthy**" (vs 47).

Jesus Christ was the "**last Adam,**" who was "**a quickening spirit**" (vs 45); He is the head of a family of men who are "**spiritual**" (vs 46); He is without sin; and He is "**the Lord from heaven**" (vs 47).

There will be no more Adams! There will only ever be two: "**the first,**" and "**the last**" (vs 45)! Jesus was sent as the head of a new family because Adam failed to head a family who worships God. Through His efforts, Jesus is the head of a family (the church) who **does** worship God!

There were only two Adams, but Adam and Jesus are called the "**first**" and "**second**" men (vs 47). There will be many more men (*men* being generic for *mankind* as God intended them to be) in God's family headed by Jesus! . . . and we know this to be the case! There have been many more men in God's family — spiritual men and women — born into the generation of Jesus Christ!

So Jesus Christ came to earth to set aright all that Adam destroyed! Jesus also came to set the example (1 Peter 2:21) for our walk in this world before God!

God saw that mankind had a major problem, compliments of Adam, and He sent Jesus to fix it! . . . and He did!

Now, those who believe in Jesus Christ can look forward to eternity in the very presence of God and His Son Jesus Christ! That is a wonderful prospect for each of us who believe!

What a gracious and merciful God we have!

32

A New Start
with Forgiven Man

As we noted in the previous chapter, sinful man can be forgiven by God and restored to a place in God's family. Through Jesus' death on the cross in payment for our sins, and His resurrection by God, we can now have our spirits quickened to God!

When Adam ate the forbidden fruit, he didn't instantly die a physical death, but his spirit, which had previously been alive to God, died instantly. Fellowship with God was ruined when Adam's spirit died to God. That is the state of man which Adam passed along to all of his descendants. Compliments of Adam, we all begin this life with a spirit which is dead to God!

When Jesus was crucified, He paid all penalties for our sins; He gave up the Ghost; He went immediately to be with God; His body was buried; and God raised His body on the third day.

Following His resurrection, He was seen by many! He was seen by well over **"five hundred brethren."** (1 Corinthians 15:5-8) After His ascension to heaven (Acts 1:9), He sat down at God's right hand. (Hebrews 10:12) His work was finished!

Jesus' actions opened the door for each of us to have newness of life — eternal life! . . . and that new life comes with a spirit which is eternally alive to God!

We cannot bring our dead spirits back to life. Only **God** can do that! . . . but God has made that possible for each of us through the work of Jesus Christ His Son!

The salvation Jesus provides to mankind is easy to obtain — yet many people believe it impossible to obtain. Salvation comes by **faith** in the Lord Jesus Christ!

"⁸**For by grace are ye saved** <u>through faith</u>**; and that not of yourselves:** <u>it is the gift of God</u>**:** ⁹**not of works, lest any man should boast.**

¹⁰**For we are** <u>His workmanship</u>**, created in Christ Jesus unto good works, which God hath before ordained that we should walk in them.**" (Ephesians 2:8-10)

Many, who refuse to believe God's Word, think we need to **work** our way to salvation. That is, they think we need to do good "**works**" to prove we are worthy. No one is worthy! Ephesians 2:8-9 teaches that salvation is by "**faith**," and not by "**works**."

Salvation is by faith, and as such, it is a **gift** from God. We believe in the redemptive work of God's Son, and He gives us salvation! If it were possible to work our way into God's family — to get there by "**works**" — mankind would brag about it! . . . and there is nothing to brag about regarding salvation!

A person who has received newness of life is "<u>**His** workmanship</u>"! . . . that is, **God's** workmanship! . . . and such a person is created so he/she can perform good works. Salvation and life do not come from good works. Read verse 10 again. We are created by Him, in Christ Jesus, "**unto**" good works. Good works follow newness of life! They do not precede it!

The last part of verse 10 says that God meant for His people to walk in good works! God "**hath before ordained**" — that is, God decided in eternity past — that His people should walk in good works!

This sentence says the same thing: we become members of His family, and then we walk in good works. It does **not** say that if we walk in good works, we will become members of His family. It doesn't work that way! God hath before ordained that all who **are** His people — **will** walk in good works!

The result is this: through faith in the work of Jesus Christ, man can take the position God always wanted him/her to have in this life — as sons and daughters of God!

The Holy Spirit to Help

God did not leave His people helpless to flounder about. With newness of life comes the gift of the Holy Spirit, the Third Person of the Trinity.

The Holy Spirit takes up residence in the heart of each believer where He can help, guide, and teach each of us! (1 Corinthians 6:19) This means that each believer has a personal tutor, guide, and empowerer, given by God, who lives in their hearts!

Jesus explained:

"**⁷Nevertheless I tell you the truth; it is expedient for you that I go away: for if I go not away, the Comforter will not come unto you; but if I depart, I will send Him unto you.**" (John 16:7)

"**¹³Howbeit when He, the Spirit of truth, is come, <u>He will guide you into all truth</u>: for He shall not speak of Himself; but whatsoever He shall hear, that shall He speak: and <u>He will shew you things to come.</u>**

¹⁴He shall glorify Me: for He shall receive of mine, and shall shew it unto you." (John 16:13-14)

In the Old Testament, God took residence for a time in the Tabernacle in the wilderness, and in the Temple in Jerusalem. The Lord also came to earth to visit and to speak to particular persons here and there. In Jesus' day, God walked among us in the Person of the Son Jesus Christ. Today, and in all days following the day of Pentecost, the Holy Spirit of God lives in the heart of each of His people!

With the Holy Spirit in a believer's heart, we have the Spirit of God with us constantly to guide us, teach us, help us, care for us, etc.

When each believer passes out of this world, just like Jesus told the repentant thief on the cross, "**To day shalt thou be with Me in paradise,**" (Luke 23:43) he/she goes directly into the Lord's presence! Upon death, the immortal souls of believers go directly into the presence of God! No stopping anywhere along the road to heaven! No passing "Go!" to collect $200. Directly! Immediately! Absent from the body, present with the Lord! Bingo!

Upon death, however, our bodies go into the grave. In a coming day, our bodies will be resurrected and changed into heavenly bodies. Then, our souls will be united with our heavenly bodies, and we will live in our new bodies for eternity with the Lord.

Eternity

After a believer passes away, and from that point in time forward, he/she will always be with the Lord! . . . and heaven and eternity future will be wonderful! **"And God shall wipe away all tears from their eyes; and there shall be no more death, neither sorrow, nor crying, neither shall there be any more pain: for the former things are passed away."** (Revelation 21:4)

This is where God's original goal for mankind will see its fulfillment! Every believer will be with Him! This includes everyone who wanted to be a child of God, who freely chose during this life to be a child of God, who accepted the salvation provided by Jesus Christ in this lifetime! Every believer will be with Him!

Eternity future will be populated by all of the Lord's children who love Him! . . . and He will be there to love and care for them as well!

On a sad note, all who reject the Lord God in this lifetime will not be there. They will not share in the joys of eternity future in the presence of God! All those who choose, in this lifetime, to have absolutely nothing to do with God, will not be forced to have anything to do with God after death!

That is an elegant feature of the solution to the sin problem: all those who want to be God's beloved children will be with Him; all those who do **not** want to be God's beloved children will **not** be with Him!

All those of us who trusted in the Lord Jesus Christ, who love Him for His selfless act on our behalf, who want to be known as God's people, etc., will all be with Him, in His presence, for eternity!

33

Jesus' Generation

Let us consider briefly the "**generation**" of Jesus Christ. Matthew 1:1 opens the whole New Testament with this expression: "**The book of <u>the generation of Jesus Christ</u>, the son of David, the son of Abraham.**"

This means that Jesus **has** His own generation!

Isaiah asked the important question: "**Who shall declare His generation?**" (Isaiah 53:8) Why is this important?

In that chapter, Isaiah was discussing the crucifixion of Jesus Christ. Isaiah 53 contains the most important prophecy in the whole Bible. About 700 years before it happened, Isaiah presented a discussion of the crucifixion of Jesus Christ. Isaiah didn't know the name of the person he was describing, but we can fill in the name through hindsight! Isaiah was writing about the crucifixion of Jesus Christ!

Isaiah asked this question (vs 8) because Jesus Christ, the Man of whom he was speaking, "**was cut off out of the land of the living.**" (Isaiah 53:8)

Jesus was crucified in His prime — without ever having married and without ever having raised a family. Because families and descendants are so important to the children of Israel, this was a very appropriate question which Isaiah raised. . . . and if a man had no wife and no family, how can he have a generation? Good question!

Let us consider.

Jesus' Own Prophecy

Having prophesied to the disciples about future days, Jesus made a statement which was recorded by three of the four Gospel writers. Jesus told His disciples, **"Verily I say unto you, This generation shall not pass till all these things be fulfilled."** (Matthew 24:34, Mark 13:30, Luke 21:32)

To **which** generation does **"This generation"** refer?

There have been many debates over this question throughout the years, and many different explanations proffered, but there is a simple answer discussed in the Bible: Jesus was talking about His Own generation! . . . His own family!

But He had no wife! He had no children! How can He have a generation? Twice, now, we've asked this same question!

The Seed of Abraham

Consider a comment in Psalm 22, which is another Old Testament Psalm which discusses crucifixion. David wrote this Psalm a long time before death by crucifixion came into use.

Speaking of the Lord, David wrote:

"A seed shall serve Him;
It shall be accounted to the Lord for a generation." (Psalm 22:30)

Jesus was cut off on the cross in His prime, without having had a family of His own. But the Psalmist said **"a seed shall serve Him."** . . . and that **"seed" ". . . shall be accounted to the Lord for a generation."**

We have seen this word **"seed"** before. The Lord used this word several times in His promises to Abraham.

These are some of the words the Lord spoke to Abraham:

"[17]That in blessing I will bless thee, and in multiplying I will multiply thy <u>seed</u> as the stars of the heaven, and as the sand which is upon the sea shore; and thy <u>seed</u> shall possess the gate of his enemies. [18]And in thy <u>seed</u> shall all the nations of the earth be blessed; because thou hast obeyed My voice." (Genesis 22:17-18)

This blessing promises to Abraham a heavenly seed, **"as the stars of the heaven,"** an earthly seed, **"as the sand which is upon the sea shore,"** and **"Christ,"** (Galatians 3:16) the seed in whom shall **"all the nations of the earth be blessed."** (Genesis 22:18)

In Genesis 22:17, the seed which "**shall possess the gate of his enemies,**" also points to Christ!

The heavenly "seed" is the church — which is made up of believers — all of whom put their faith in Christ. "**And if ye be Christ's, then are ye Abraham's seed, and heirs according to the promise.**" (Galatians 3:29)

The earthly "seed" are the natural descendants of Abraham (the children of Israel, the Jewish people.)

Then there is the "seed" which is Jesus Christ, King of the Jews, born in the line of David. Paul explained: "**Now to Abraham and his <u>seed</u> were the promises made. He saith not, 'And to seeds,' as of many; but as of one, 'And to thy <u>seed</u>,' which is Christ.**" (Galatians 3:16)

The heavenly "seed," which is the "seed" promised to Abraham to be as innumerable as the stars of the sky (Genesis 22:17), is also the "seed" who shall "**serve Him**" — the "seed" which shall be "**accounted to the Lord for a generation.**" (Psalm 22:30)

This "seed" is the Lord Jesus Christ's generation! All those who put their faith in Him, who are adopted by God as brethren into His family, are members of His generation! . . . and "**this generation**" (Matthew 24:34) — **His** generation — will not pass away until all of Jesus' prophecies are fulfilled!

Jesus' Family

Jesus' generation, made possible by His crucifixion, is the family of man whom the Lord God has been seeking all throughout history. Jesus' family, "**this generation,**" will last throughout all eternity! His generation won't ever pass away!

Jesus' generation will be comprised of all mankind who want to spend eternity with, and in the care of, the loving God! These people want to fellowship with God, and they will be honored and privileged to be able to fellowship with the Lord God and Jesus Christ — for eternity!

This is what free will in mankind has allowed! Those who want nothing to do with the Lord God, and with His Son Jesus Christ, will get their wish! They won't be forced to spend any time at all with God!

But all those members of mankind who want to dwell with God and be His people, they will be with Him throughout all eternity! Jesus' generation represents the fulfillment of God's will for mankind!

Jesus made **this generation** possible by paying all penalties for all sins of all mankind! . . . and the Lord God can forgive each of us who puts his/her faith in the Lord Jesus Christ. He can welcome us all into His presence, because all penalties for our sins have been paid-in-full! God's righteousness, which demands payment for sins committed, has been fully satisfied! All believers are in! . . . and God's righteousness has been satisfied!

Jesus was born of king David's house, which the Lord said He would establish for ever. Jesus Christ is King in the line of David! . . . and that title and kingdom are His for ever! Through Jesus Christ, God has established David's house for ever!

God's promises to Abraham have all been fulfilled! All that remains is the day of Jesus' return to earth — His second coming — when He will gather all of His children unto Himself! . . . and that day will be soon!

Notice that God's great desire for creating mankind — to have a people of His own with whom He can fellowship for all eternity — has been made possible by the work of His Son Jesus Christ! God's great desire will be fulfilled!

Adam didn't represent God well by sinning almost immediately! . . . but Jesus **did** represent God well! . . . and through Jesus' work on the cross, God will have a people of His own whom He can love, fellowship, care, guide, communicate, enjoy, etc., for ever!

34

Sin and the Adversary
Are Defeated

The main adversary to mankind in this world is Satan, also known as the devil. He was present as the serpent in the garden of Eden. He enticed Eve to eat of the forbidden fruit; she gave some to Adam; and Adam disobeyed the Lord's command when he took a bite.

Adam's sin, against the Lord's direct command, brought death into the world. **"For the wages of sin is death; but the gift of God is eternal life through Jesus Christ our Lord."** (Romans 6:23)

Jesus Freed Us from Sin

Those who put their faith in Jesus Christ have been freed from sin! Those who reject Jesus Christ remain in their sin!

All those who are freed from sin have become **"the servants of righteousness unto holiness."**

"¹⁷But God be thanked, that ye were the servants of sin, but ye have obeyed from the heart that form of doctrine which was delivered you. ¹⁸Being then made free from sin, ye became the servants of righteousness unto holiness." (Romans 6:17-18)

The next verse also indicates that believers have been made free from sin. . . . and once freed from sin, believers become **"servants to God,"** producing fruit which is holy. This all leads to eternal life.

"But now being made free from sin, and become servants to God, ye had your fruit unto holiness, and the end everlasting life." (Romans 6:22)

As Great High Priest, Jesus Christ did not enter into holy places made by man (for example, the Tabernacle and the Temple), but He entered into "heaven itself," "to appear in the presence of God for us." . . . and He only had to do this ONCE! "In the end of the world," Jesus entered the very presence of God once "to put away sin by the sacrifice of Himself." That He only needed to do this once is very important!

A perfect sacrifice only needs to be made once. All those sacrifices which are not perfect, which are only figures of the perfect, must be made over and over and over again.

Jesus entered into God's very presence "to put away sin" by His sacrifice "of Himself"! When He did this, He freed us from sin! How? He put away sin!

Here is the whole passage:

"24For Christ is not entered into the holy places made with hands, which are the figures of the true; but into heaven itself, now to appear in the presence of God for us:

25Nor yet that He should offer Himself often, as the high priest entereth into the holy place every year with blood of others; 26for then must He often have suffered since the foundation of the world: but now once in the end of the world hath He appeared to put away sin by the sacrifice of Himself." (Hebrews 9:24-26)

Furthermore, Jesus not only freed us from sin, and put away sin, He cleansed us from all sin!

"But if we walk in the light, as He is in the light, we have fellowship one with another, and the blood of Jesus Christ His Son cleanseth us from all sin." (1 John 1:7)

Jesus accomplished all of this when He was crucified on the cross of Calvary for the sins of all mankind.

Jesus Destroyed the Devil

In that selfless act, Jesus destroyed the devil!

What are the devil's characteristics? He is a murderer; he abides not in the truth; there is no truth in him; he is a liar; and he is the father of all lies!

Jesus told the Jews the following:

"**Ye are of your father the devil, and the lusts of your father ye will do. He was a murderer from the beginning, and abode not in the truth, because there is no truth in him. When he speaketh a lie, he speaketh of his own: for he is a liar, and the father of it.**" (John 8:44)

The devil is the adversary of all mankind, especially of all those who believe in the Lord Jesus Christ, because he is the adversary of the Lord Jesus Christ! Peter described the devil as "**a roaring lion,**" "**seeking whom he may devour.**" The devil is a very dangerous creature!

"**Be sober, be vigilant; because your adversary the devil, as a roaring lion, walketh about, seeking whom he may devour.**" (1 Peter 5:8)

A main purpose for the Son of God coming to earth as a man was to "**destroy the works of the devil.**" That task is not within the capabilities of natural man. The more powerful of the two — natural man or the devil — is the devil. He will win every battle with natural man!

But the more powerful of the two — the Lord Jesus Christ or the devil — is the Lord Jesus Christ! . . . and when He died on the cross, He destroyed the works of the devil — which are SIN and DEATH!

"**He that committeth sin is of the devil; for the devil sinneth from the beginning. For this purpose the Son of God was manifested, that He might destroy the works of the devil.**" (1 John 3:8)

Ultimately, the devil will be cast into the lake of fire for all eternity. When he is finally there, he will no longer be a threat to mankind! (Revelation 20:10) All this was made possible when Jesus sacrificed Himself on the cross of Calvary for **every** man. (Hebrews 2:9)

Summary

Jesus cleansed all believers from sin, and He destroyed the works of the devil when He was crucified for the sins of the world!

Jesus' actions made it possible for all mankind (every man, woman, and child) to come into the presence of God! He made it possible for mankind to fellowship with God as His people, and for God to love, care for, and fellowship with a family of His own!

Jesus made it possible for God to have His desired family relationship with the sons and daughters of man!

35

Paul As An Example

Let's look at some examples of men of God from the New Testament. When we were looking at Adam, Noah, the patriarchs, the children of Israel, the judges, and the Old Testament kings of Judah and Israel, the general direction of their relationships to the Lord was downhill. Many of them appeared to be good men, but as they sinned, they descended lower and lower into sin and depravity, and grew further and further away from the Lord.

Consider king Solomon. He started out really great! . . . but then towards the end of his life, he fell away from the Lord into idolatry.

In contrast, New Testament believers like Saul started out as sinners, evil scoundrels, murderers, and enemies of Jesus Christ. Through faith in Jesus, however, these men became servants of Christ. As Christians, their characters became more and more Christ-like, and they rose to higher and higher levels of holiness.

Character in Old Testament times for descendants of Adam went down, down, down under the influences of the world, the flesh, and the devil. Character and spirituality for all believers in New Testament times goes up, up, up under the influence and empowerment of the Holy Spirit! This is a mighty contrast!

Saul of Tarsus

When we are first introduced to Saul of Tarsus, he was an evil man. When Stephen was stoned, Saul stood there watching — in full agreement with the mob. Those who stoned Stephen laid their clothes at

187

the feet of their leader, Saul who, as the man-in-charge, was not about to get his own hands dirty. (Acts 7:58)

A few verses later, we read, "**And Saul was consenting unto his death.**" (Acts 8:1) Saul was perfectly fine with the stoning of Stephen.

What else do we know about Saul?

"**As for Saul, he made havock of the church, entering into every house, and haling men and women committed them to prison.**" (Acts 8:3)

To hale men and women means *to drag them out* of their houses and haul them before the authorities. Saul was an enemy of all Christians.

Saul was educated as a Pharisee who were a highly educated sect of the Jews of that day. Because Saul was an educated man, he was well-versed in the Mosaic law.

There is more:

"**¹And Saul, yet breathing out threatenings and slaughter against the disciples of the Lord, went unto the high priest, ²and desired of him letters to Damascus to the synagogues , that if he found any of this way, whether they were men or women, he might bring them bound unto Jerusalem.**" (Acts 9:1-2)

Not only was Saul an evil enemy of all Christians, but he was an **ambitious** evil enemy of all Christians! He didn't sit back and wait for the priests to come to him to search for followers of "**this way,**" which was their word for *Christianity*. He went to the priests seeking letters of authorization to search for and destroy believers!

In Saul's day, he was considered a monster! Saul's name would fit well into a list of the most evil men of recent times! He was that bad!

Saul Encounters Jesus Christ

In the days well after the crucifixion, resurrection, and ascension of Jesus Christ, as Saul was traveling on the Damascus road, the Lord Jesus Christ confronted him!

"**³And as he journeyed, he came near Damascus: and suddenly there shined round about him a light from heaven: ⁴and he fell to the earth, and heard a voice saying unto him, 'Saul, Saul, why persecuteth thou Me?'** " (Acts 9:3-4)

When he saw the bright light and heard the voice, he immediately fell to the earth and asked, "**Who art Thou, Lord?**" Jesus identified

Himself: "**I am Jesus whom thou persecutest: it is hard for thee to kick against the pricks.**" (Acts 9:5)

Clarke[7] explained that the comment, "**it is hard for thee to kick against the pricks,**" "signifies the fruitlessness and absurdity of rebelling against lawful authority."

That explains it very well! Paul was fighting a losing battle against the Lord Jesus Christ and his protestations were accomplishing nothing!

When Saul heard Jesus' reply, we read, "**And he trembling and astonished said, 'Lord, what wilt Thou have me to do?' And the Lord said unto him, 'Arise, and go into the city, and it shall be told thee what thou must do.'** " (Acts 9:6)

Saul immediately recognized Jesus! . . . and he understood exactly what Jesus' words meant! He knew this was the man they crucified; he knew he was in the wrong; and he knew he was bowed down before the very Lord God of the universe! All this occurred in an instant!

When he rose, he was blind! His men had to lead him into the city. One encounter with Jesus, and this formerly powerful man was totally helpless! One encounter and he knew he stood before the Lord God! . . . and he knew he was **guilty** of numerous terrible sins committed against the Lord and His people!

Fortunately for Saul, Jesus is a forgiving God, unlike Saul who was not forgiving of the believers he had encountered.

Jesus' Words to Saul

The Lord told Ananias He wanted him to go speak to Saul. Ananias was afraid because he knew Saul's reputation! You can almost hear Ananias thinking, "Riiiiiight!!! You want me to go talk to Saul!" The Lord assured him, however, that it would be safe.

"[15]**But the Lord said unto him, 'Go thy way: for he is a chosen vessel unto Me, to bear My name before the Gentiles, and kings, and the children of Israel:** [16]**for I will shew him how great things he must suffer for My name's sake.**" (Acts 9:15-16)

Note in this passage that the Lord told Ananias exactly what He expected Saul to do in His service. As "**a chosen vessel**" unto the Lord, Saul would:

- "**bear My name before the Gentiles,**"
- "**bear My name before . . . kings,**"

- "bear My name before . . . the children of Israel," and
- "suffer" "great things for My name's sake."

Saul was going to carry the Lord's name before Gentiles, kings, and the children of Israel, and suffer all the while he was doing it! Saul had caused many Christians to suffer, and now, it was his turn to be on the receiving end of evil men like his former self!

So Ananias went and spoke with Saul.

"¹⁷And Ananias went his way, and entered into the house; and putting his hands on him said, 'Brother Saul, the Lord, even Jesus, that appeared unto thee in the way as thou camest, hath sent me, that thou mightest receive thy sight, and be filled with the Holy Ghost.'

¹⁸And immediately there fell from his eyes as it had been scales: and he received sight forthwith, and arose, and was baptized." (Acts 9:17-18)

Note that Luke also tells us why the Lord sent Ananias unto Saul. Ananias was there to assure Saul:

- "that thou mightest receive thy sight," and
- "that thou mightest . . . be filled with the Holy Ghost."

Ananias was assigned to help Saul, to explain to him what was happening, and to tell him what he was to do in the Lord's service!

Saul received his sight. In addition, he was "filled with the Holy Ghost." He had believed that Jesus was the Christ in the instant the Lord stopped him along the Damascus road. Here, with Ananias, he was beginning to be outfitted for his service to the Lord!

When Saul rose up, he asked to be baptized! He went from being an enemy of Christ to a follower of Christ in an instant! . . . and it appears he understood quite well — because he immediately asked to be baptized. He wanted to make a statement as soon as possible before the watching world that he was a follower of Jesus Christ!

For those who believe salvation is based on works, we must ask: What had Saul done for Jesus Christ before he was saved? The answer to that question is: Nothing! Saul was an enemy of Jesus Christ! . . . and an especially vicious enemy of Christ at that!

When he was confronted by Jesus Christ, he was blinded and made helpless by that single encounter! Saul couldn't **do** anything then, either! He immediately believed in the Lord; everything he had learned about the Lord from his Pharisaical training fit into its proper place; and he understood! Then, he received the Holy Spirit; he was baptized; and he received his first marching orders! No works whatsoever up to this point! Just faith!

When next we see Saul, he was preaching Christ! Works are a **result** of salvation, not a prerequisite to it!

"**And straightway he preached Christ in the synagogues, that He is the Son of God.**" (Acts 9:20)

The light bulb had flashed on in Saul's mind! All the blanks from his religious training had been filled in by the Lord Jesus Christ — in an instant!

Why Saul?

The conversion of Saul shows us that anyone — even an evil monster like Saul — can turn their lives over to the Lord! Who would believe someone like Saul could actually be saved? Who would believe that Hitler, Stalin, Lenin, or Mao, could ever be saved?

Saul's conversion shows that even the worst criminals can be saved! The other four evil men mentioned did **not** turn their lives over to the Lord before their deaths. They could have, but they didn't! . . . but Saul, who fits well in that list of evil men, **did** put his faith in the Lord! . . . and if Saul can be saved — then anybody can be saved!

Ananias didn't believe it initially! His reaction to Saul's salvation mirrors our reactions if we heard that any of the other four evil men had been saved.

Before he was saved, Saul was ambitious towards capturing and torturing Christians. After he was saved, Paul was an equally ambitious servant of the Lord under the empowerment of the Holy Spirit! He demonstrated this in his preaching of the Good News of the Gospel of Jesus Christ to unbelievers! In fact, Saul, later to be known as Paul, was one of the greatest Christians who ever lived!

Paul, Servant of Jesus Christ

Luke, the author of Acts, did not make a big deal of Saul's name change. One minute he was Saul, the next he was Paul.

"**Then Saul, (who also is called Paul,) filled with the Holy Ghost, . . .**" (Acts 13:9)

We saw in the Old Testament that when Pharaohnechoh made Eliakim king of Judah, he changed his name to Jehoiakim. (2 Kings 23:34) This showed that Pharaohnechoh was in charge. That is, pharaoh held power over Jehoiakim, and he changed his name to show everyone who was in charge.

The Lord did not need to demonstrate His power over Saul by changing his name to Paul. It is likely, however, that the Lord changed Saul's name to Paul based upon the meanings of the two names.

The name *Saul* means "Asked for." (Newberry Bible, margin, 1 Samuel 9:2) The name *Paul* means "Little." (Strong's)

This name change is very telling! **Saul** was very popular among the people! . . . evil, but popular! . . . and the people **asked for** him regularly — consistent with the meaning of his name.

But when Saul gave his life to Christ, he became *little* in his own eyes. His new name **Paul** was very appropriate for his new life in Christ!

Saul wanted everyone to look up to him! He was really hot stuff! . . . but Paul wanted everyone to look up to the Lord Jesus Christ. Saul wanted his own efforts as a persecutor of Christians to be exalted! Paul, however, wanted his service to the Lord to fade into the background so the Lord Jesus Christ would be exalted!

Paul asked the following question which shows his attitude towards himself:

"**²⁴O wretched man that I am! Who shall deliver me from the body of this death?**

²⁵I thank God through Jesus Christ our Lord." (Romans 7:24-25)

Does calling oneself "**O wretched man,**" sound like Saul? No! . . . but it is completely consistent with Paul's new attitude! Who would deliver this wretched man? (vs 24) The answer lies in verse 25, "**God through Jesus Christ our Lord,**" would deliver him! Paul knew exactly from whom he had received salvation! . . . and Paul was thankful for it! This is completely consistent with Paul's new attitude and his new life in Christ!

Paul's Service to the Lord

Paul spent the rest of his life as a servant of Jesus Christ preaching the Gospel to Jews and Gentiles alike! He traveled widely throughout the region, preaching the Gospel everywhere he went. Ultimately, Paul went to Rome. After years of house arrest, all the while preaching to the citizens and visitors in Rome, and writing letters of teaching and encouragement to the churches he had visited, Paul was put to death!

During those years of service, he wrote many letters which are included in the Canon of the Bible. The epistles to the Romans, Corinthians, Galatians, Ephesians, Philippians, Colossians, Thessalonians, Timothy, Titus, and Philemon are all Paul's writings.

Officially, the author of the book of Hebrews is unknown, but it sounds very much like Paul's writing, too. Hebrews explains how Jesus Christ fits into, meshes perfectly with, and fulfills the Mosaic law of the Jewish religion. Having been trained a Pharisee, Paul was intimately acquainted with the Old Testament law! The letter to Hebrews fits well with Paul's experience, education, and understanding.

As mentioned earlier, Paul was one of the greatest Christians who ever lived! . . . even though he started his adult life as one of the most evil and most feared persecutors of Christians who ever lived!

Paul set the tone for all Christians to follow. On one occasion, he said, **"For I reckon that the sufferings of this present time are not worthy to be compared with the glory which shall be revealed in us."** (Romans 8:18)

Following his conversion, Paul's eyes were constantly on his Lord Jesus Christ! If we all could follow in his footsteps as devoted followers, friends, and servants of the Lord Jesus Christ, that would be just wonderful!

In Paul, the Lord found a follower with whom He could have great fellowship! . . . and that aspect of Paul's life is a great example to each of us!

36

Stephen As An Example

Stephen was the first Christian martyr. We know considerably less about Stephen's early life than we knew about Paul's, but Stephen's story is nevertheless very powerful.

The fact that we know little about Stephen's early life suggests that he could be a picture of any of us! The story picks up after Stephen believed and was a disciple and a servant of Jesus Christ! His life as a believer should speak mightily to all of us!

Stephen's Life

When the early Christians needed someone to care for the widows who were being **"neglected in the daily ministration"** (Acts 6:1), the Apostles set out to identify men qualified to take charge of this ministry.

The criteria for these men are listed in Acts 6:3: **"Wherefore brethren, look ye out among you seven men of honest report, full of the Holy Ghost and wisdom, whom we may appoint over this business."**

They wanted to identify seven men who were:
- of honest report,
- full of the Holy Ghost, and
- full of wisdom.

The first person identified was Stephen, **"a man full of faith and of the Holy Ghost."** (Acts 6:5)

A few verses later, Luke described Stephen again:

"And Stephen, full of faith and power, did great wonders and miracles among the people." (Acts 6:8)

Stephen was a powerful servant of the Lord whose service was to help those in need.

Certain men of the synagogue, however, disputed with Stephen's words. . . . but **"they were not able to resist the wisdom and the spirit by which he spake."** (Acts 6:10) The Holy Spirit was with Stephen, so the men of the synagogue could not resist his words! Why? . . . because when Stephen spoke, the Holy Spirit supplied him with great words of wisdom!

The Accusations Against Stephen

Since those in the synagogues were not able to resist **"the wisdom and the spirit"** by which Stephen spoke, they **"suborned"** men. *To suborn* is "to induce secretly to do an unlawful thing." (Webster's)

That is, they found men willing to give false testimony against Stephen. **"Then they suborned men, which said, 'We have heard him speak blasphemous words against Moses, and against God.'"** (Acts 6:11) The simplest way to express this? The witnesses lied! These were Jews who were speaking against a believer in Jesus Christ!

But they didn't just give false testimony. **"And they stirred up the people, and the elders, and the scribes, and came upon him, and caught him, and brought him to the council."** (Acts 6:12) They stirred up everybody emotionally, caught Stephen, and dragged him before the council!

Once he was before the council, they had men present more false testimony against him! **"[13]And set up false witnesses, which said, 'This man ceaseth not to speak blasphemous words against this holy place, and the law: [14]for we have heard him say, that this Jesus of Nazareth shall destroy this place, and shall change the customs which Moses delivered.'"** (Acts 6:13-14)

These false witnesses labeled every word from Stephen's mouth a lie! They accused him of lying against the Temple and the law! They misquoted some of his words simply because they did not understand. Jesus did say, **"destroy the temple of God,"** (Matthew 26:61), but He was speaking about His own body, not about the Temple building in Jerusalem. Stephen had accurately quoted the Lord's words, and these false witnesses didn't understand His meaning.

The really blasphemous words and lies on that occasion were the words spoken by the false witnesses before the council. All of their accusations against Stephen were falsehoods because their words were either outright lies or only partial truths! They totally misunderstood Jesus' and Stephen's actual words, and for that reason, their accusations came out as twisted versions of the truth.

How was Stephen taking all of this?

"And all that sat in the council, looking stedfastly on him, saw his face as it had been the face of an angel." (Acts 6:15)

Stephen took it well because he knew he was in the right! He was especially calm because he knew the Lord was with him! It is hard to believe such a description could apply to any man considering the emotional nature of the whole scene! ... but it accurately characterized Stephen's face and demeanor! In the midst of chaos, Stephen remained quite calm — angelic even!

Stephen's Defense

If the council did not want to hear the truth, they should not have allowed Stephen to speak in his own defense. But they did!

They asked Stephen if the false testimonies were true. ... and he started his defense with a historical review — starting with the Lord's words to Abraham. Remember, Stephen was speaking to Jewish leaders, so they should easily have followed his words.

Jewish History

Stephen began with the history of Abraham, Isaac, Jacob, and the twelve tribes of Israel. Then, he told how Jacob's sons sold their own brother Joseph into slavery in Egypt. Stephen declared that Joseph may have been separated from his family and his brothers, **"but God was with him."** (Acts 7:9)

He told how God set up Joseph to be **"governor over Egypt and all his house."** (Acts 7:10) ... and when a great, seven-year famine hit the whole region, Joseph had stored enough food during the years of plenty, to feed all the people of Egypt as well as people from many other lands!

When Joseph's family in Canaan learned that the Egyptians had stored plenty of food, they traveled there to purchase some. When they learned that it was Joseph, their brother, who was in charge, they all moved to Egypt to live out the duration of the famine. During their sojourn in

Egypt, which lasted well beyond the time of famine, the children of Israel multiplied greatly! Even though they had become slaves to the Egyptians, their numbers continued to increase.

Then, Moses was born to a Hebrew family. By an interesting set of circumstances, he came to grow up in the house of pharaoh. When he became an adult, he killed an Egyptian who was fighting with a Hebrew. This caused him to flee the country. The Lord God, however, chose Moses to lead His people out of bondage in Egypt. . . . and the Lord sent him back to Egypt.

With reference to Moses' words, Stephen then added this:

"This is that Moses, which said unto the children of Israel, 'A prophet shall the Lord your God raise up unto you of your brethren, like unto me; Him shall ye hear.' " (Acts 7:37)

This was a quote from Deuteronomy 18:15, with which all the Jews at Stephen's hearing should have been familiar! He continued to explain about Moses' experiences with the Lord God.

"[38]**This is he, that was in the church in the wilderness with the angel which spake to him in the mount Sina, and with our fathers: who received the lively oracles to give unto us:** [39]**to whom our fathers would not obey, but thrust him from them, and in their hearts turned back again into Egypt,** [40]**saying unto Aaron, 'Make us gods to go before us: for as for this Moses, which brought us out of the land of Egypt, we wot not what is become of him.' "** (Acts 7:38-40)

The "prophet" (vs 37) of whom the Lord spoke, was the one who resided in the Tabernacle (vs 38), who rescued them from Egypt (vs 40), who spoke with their fathers (vs 38), who gave them the law (vs 38), whom their fathers would not obey (vs 39), and whom their fathers thrust from them, desiring rather in their hearts to return to Egypt (vs 39)!

The men at Stephen's hearing should have been familiar with, and understood, all of this! Their fathers among the children of Israel, were the very ones who told Aaron to make them a golden idol because they did not know what had happened to Moses. That claim was ridiculous because at that very time, Moses was exactly where they last saw him — up on mount Sinai speaking with God — on their behalf!

In response, Aaron made them a golden calf, to which they offered sacrifice, and **"rejoiced in the works of their own hands."** (vs 41)

Stephen told them that God **"gave them up to worship the host of heaven,"** (vs 42) and all manner of other heathen idols! Stephen mentioned Molech and Remphan as two gods which they worshipped. After seeing such abominations, God gave them into the hands of the Babylonians to be carried off into captivity in Babylon. (vs 43)

Stephen recounted that king David wanted to build a house for the Lord, **"But Solomon built Him an house."** (vs 47) He accurately added that the Most High doesn't dwell in houses built by the hands of man! (vs 48) Then to support this, Stephen quoted the Lord's words from Isaiah 66:1-2:

"⁴⁹Heaven is My throne

And earth is My footstool:

What house will ye build Me? saith the Lord:

Or what is the place of My rest?

⁵⁰Hath not My hand made all these things?" (Acts 7:49-50)

Everything to this point should have been most familiar to the Jewish leaders of the day! Read the full account of Stephen's words in Acts 7, to gain a complete picture of his speech!

His Rebuke of the Jewish Council

From here on, however, Stephen rebuked the council for their behavior — which they did not like at all! He considered the men of the council to be of the same minds as the children of Israel he had just described. His evaluation was quite accurate!

"⁵¹Ye stiffnecked and uncircumcised in heart and ears, ye do always resist the Holy Ghost: as your fathers did, so do ye. ⁵²Which of the prophets have not your fathers persecuted? and they have slain them which shewed before of the coming of the Just One; of whom ye have been now the betrayers and murderers: ⁵³who have received the law by the disposition of angels, and have not kept it." (Acts 8:51-53)

Stephen accused them of:

- being stiffnecked,
- being uncircumcised in heart,
- being uncircumcised in ears, and
- always resisting the Holy Ghost.

Not only did Stephen accuse those present in the council that day, but he accused their fathers also:

- of persecuting the prophets,
- of killing those who spoke of the coming of the Just One,

- of betraying the Just One,
- of murdering the Just One,
- of receiving the law from angels, but
- of not keeping it!

Their response to Stephen's accusations and rebuke was violent: **"When they heard these things, they were cut to the heart, and they gnashed on him with their teeth."** (Acts 7:54)

Stephen had hit a major nerve! . . . but during this time, look how Luke described Stephen:

"⁵⁵But he, being full of the Holy Ghost, looked up stedfastly into heaven, and saw the glory of God, and Jesus standing on the right hand of God, ⁵⁶and said, 'Behold, I see the heavens opened, and the Son of man standing on the right hand of God.' " (Acts 7:55-56)

Stephen was filled with the Holy Ghost! All of his words of rebuke — all of his accusations — were empowered by the Holy Spirit of God and they were 100% accurate!

Note also that Stephen saw "**Jesus <u>standing</u> on the right hand of God.**" He looked up, saw Jesus standing there, and he described out loud what he saw so all those in the council understood what he was seeing!

To claim such a thing as this most probably incensed them! They must have thought it was absurd that such a lowly man as Stephen could actually be seeing such things!

We know, from the book of Hebrews that Jesus is seated at the right hand of God. Hebrews 1:3 says that Jesus, when He "**had by Himself purged our sins, sat down on the right hand of the Majesty on high.**"

Hebrews 10:12 says, "**But this man, after He had offered one sacrifice for sins for ever, sat down on the right hand of God.**"

Stephen, however, saw Jesus standing! This was emphasized by repetition in Acts 7:55,56!

The Lord Jesus Christ sat down on the right hand of God when His work was completed! That is where we find Him today — seated at the right hand of God!

But when one of His saints is about to arrive, as Stephen was about to do, the Lord Jesus Christ stands up to receive and welcome His brethren into heaven! That is wonderful to know!

The Jewish Leaders' Response

We saw in verse 54, that they were "**cut to the heart,**" and "**they gnashed on him with their teeth.**" They were seriously and violently upset by his words! There was even more reaction from them:

"**⁵⁷Then they cried out with a loud voice, and stopped their ears, and ran upon him with one accord, ⁵⁸and cast him out of the city, and stoned him: . . .**" (Acts 57-58)

In their rage, they did not want to hear any more of his words. . . . and they were unified in that rage! So they cast him out of the city and put him to death!

We might ask: Who was their leader? The rest of verse 58 gives that answer: ". . . **and the witnesses laid down their clothes at a young man's feet, whose name was Saul.**"

Those who stoned Stephen put their clothes at Saul's feet. The man in charge of the detail, who doesn't want to get his own hands dirty, stands back, watches, and lets others do the dirty work! While doing that, he kept an eye on their clothes which they also didn't want to get dirty!

Paul admitted in Acts 22:20, "**And when the blood of thy martyr Stephen was shed, I also was standing by, and consenting unto his death, and kept the raiment of them that slew him.**"

Stephen's Final Words

But Stephen wasn't finished speaking:

"**⁵⁹And they stoned Stephen, calling upon God, and saying, 'Lord Jesus, receive my spirit.' ⁶⁰And he kneeled down, and cried with a loud voice, 'Lord, lay not this sin to their charge.' And when he had said this, he fell asleep.**" (Acts 7:59-60)

The act of stoning is a bloody, cruel, gruesome sight to watch! . . . and whether or not they wanted to hear any more from Stephen, surely they heard his last words!

He called upon the Lord to receive his spirit. It seems to be a rather calm request, even though the scene was anything but calm! . . . and his last words were a loud cry! "**Lord, lay not this sin to their charge.**"

Saul was standing there watching and listening to all of this! Just think of the great testimony, and influence Stephen's last words had on Saul!

The story of Stephen's martyrdom (Acts 7) is followed in relatively short order by more descriptions of Saul (Acts 8), and Saul's conversion. (Acts 9)

Saul clearly heard how Stephen reviewed the history of the children of Israel from Abraham's day forward — including his mention of the "**Prophet**" from Deuteronomy (18:15) who was Jesus Christ, the man they had just crucified! As a Pharisee, Saul was familiar with all of the details Stephen presented! Saul heard the accusations and the rebuke, empowered by the Holy Spirit through the mouth of Stephen! . . . and Saul heard Stephen's plea for forgiveness for his killers!

None of us was present that day, obviously, but the account Luke gives of this event in Acts 7 is powerful, emotional, and influential! Just reading it is enough to cause us to say, "Wow! What a man of God!"

Saul clearly saw behavior which was totally unusual for natural man! . . . and he had run roughshod over many believers, so he must had heard many similar testimonies! Maybe none more powerful on his soul than that which he witnessed here with Stephen, but the cumulative effect surely must have had a major influence on him!

Children of the Lord

This account of Stephen's martyrdom shows the bond believers have with the Lord! It shows the strength, power, and calm the Lord provides to those in His service! . . . and it shows the close relationship believers have with the Lord Jesus Christ, and with God the Father!

This demonstrates the strength of fellowship God always wanted to have with a people of His own! . . . and it shows the level of love men, women, and children can have with their Lord, Jesus Christ!

It also shows the strength the Holy Spirit provides to the Lord's children when they find themselves in harm's way at the hands of natural man! Apart from the strength the Holy Spirit provides, we would never see anything from natural man that comes even close to this!

In the calmness and serenity he enjoyed in his last minutes on earth, Stephen was Christ-like! Stephen's martyrdom is an extremely powerful testimony to all!

37

Peter As An Example

Peter's Call

Peter was an interesting character who was very different from Paul and Stephen. Peter was a fisherman whom Jesus called to be an Apostle. Paul was not one of the twelve, but he met Jesus on the Damascus Road after His resurrection and ascension. Stephen was not one of the twelve either, although he might have been one of Jesus' disciples before, during, and after his crucifixion. We don't know those details.

In Peter's case, at the start of Jesus' ministry, Jesus walked up to him one day by the sea and said, "**Follow Me**"! . . . and Peter followed Him! . . . just like that!

"**18And Jesus, walking by the sea of Galilee, saw two brethren, Simon called Peter, and Andrew his brother, casting a net into the sea: for they were fishers. 19And He saith unto them, 'Follow Me, and I will make you fishers of men.' 20And they straightway left their nets, and followed him.**" (Matthew 4:18-20)

Saul, who spent his time persecuting Christians, needed to be confronted by the power of Jesus Christ! He saw a bright light, heard a great voice, and was blinded when Jesus Christ confronted him. (Acts 9)

Peter only needed to hear one quiet command from the Lord Jesus: "**Follow Me**"! . . . and he followed! Remember: this happened at the very beginning of Jesus' ministry, well before He was crucified! Stephen and Paul only enter the picture after the crucifixion, resurrection, and day of Pentecost.

In Saul's case, Jesus needed to confront him, identify Himself, and only then did Saul believe. We don't know how it went with Stephen.

Everyone is different. Some people hear about Jesus and they obey easily and quickly. Some people need a stronger encounter to convince them. Some people (like Judas Iscariot) never give in — ever — and remain stubbornly opposed to the end! Each of us needs to hear Jesus' call and respond according to our own temperament. Hopefully, we won't respond like Judas Iscariot did!

Peter's Temperament

Paul was an educated, dynamic individual. Peter, on the other hand, was a fisherman who generally spoke first and thought later. This author's father-in-law always described Peter as the first person with the ailment known as 'foot-in-mouth' disease.

Peter was an emotional person. The combination of his emotions and his quickness of speech got him into frequent trouble.

Nevertheless, Peter had one of the closest relationships to Jesus of any of the Apostles.

Peter's Identification of Jesus Christ

Following the feeding of the five thousand, Jesus asked His disciples who the people thought He was. They suggested that some thought He was John the Baptist, some Elijah, and some one of the Old Testament prophets. Then Jesus asked for their own answer:

"He said unto them, 'But whom say ye that I am?' Peter answering said, 'The Christ of God.' " (Luke 9:20)

Peter knew exactly who Jesus was!   . . . and in private conversations, he had no problem expressing his clear understanding.

On The Mount of Transfiguration

When Jesus went up onto the mountain to be transfigured (Matthew 17), He took Peter, James, and John with Him. This was a high honor for the three Apostles, and it is an indication of the close relationship the three men enjoyed with the Lord Jesus.

On the mountain, Moses and Elijah (Elias) appeared and talked with Jesus. With such an opportunity to witness this special occasion, one would think everyone would be quiet, watch, listen, learn, and appreciate the privilege of being an invited witness. But Peter spoke up!

"**⁴Then answered Peter, and said unto Jesus, 'Lord, it is good for us to be here: if Thou wilt, let us make here three tabernacles; one for Thee, and one for Moses, and one for Elias.'**

⁵While he yet spake, behold, a bright cloud overshadowed them: and behold, a voice out of the cloud, which said, 'This is My beloved Son, in whom I am well pleased; hear ye Him.'

⁶And when the disciples heard it, they fell on their face, and were sore afraid. ⁷And Jesus came and touched them, and said, 'Arise, and be not afraid.' " (Matthew 17:4-7)

It appears that God told Peter that day, "Be quiet! . . . and listen to Jesus!" Clearly, God's words are applicable to all of us! . . . but Peter was the one who was talking when he should have been listening.

This was a wonderful moment for the three Apostles to be there to see Moses and Elijah, to hear God's words concerning His Son, and to witness the transfiguration of the Son of God! Such an experience like this certainly had a strengthening influence on the faith of each of these three men!

Peter's Three Denials of Jesus

Another event which gives insight into the quick tongue of Peter was his three-time denial of the Lord Jesus prior to His crucifixion. Luke recorded this story.

Jesus had just told Peter that Satan desired to have Peter on his side. . . . and Jesus had just prayed to the Father, asking that Peter's faith would not fail in that trial. Then Jesus encouraged Peter, suggesting that after he was converted, he should "**strengthen thy brethren.**" (Luke 22:31-32)

Jesus knew the Holy Spirit had not yet come upon Peter, so he needed strength and help. Jesus understood the status of all of the Apostles who were still operating without the Holy Spirit. . . . but Peter did not yet understand!

As if to indicate how strong he was, Peter then told Jesus, "**Lord, I am ready to go with Thee, both into prison, and to death.**" (Luke 22:33)

Peter's heart was in the right place, but he did not understand the truly frail nature of mankind. He needed to learn! . . . and on this occasion, he spoke these words rather quickly, without giving much thought to their ramifications.

The Lord then answered Peter with these famous words: **"And He said, 'I tell thee, Peter, the cock shall not crow this day, before that thou shalt thrice deny that thou knowest Me.' "** (Luke 22:34)

Peter was about to learn how really weak he was. He certainly didn't think he was weak; he thought he was a staunch supporter of Jesus Christ; he thought he could stand up to anything; but he would learn!

When they took Jesus away for the trial, Peter followed at a distance. (Luke 22:54) They lit a fire in the hall, and everyone, including Peter, sat down around it. (Luke 22:55)

Denial #1

"⁵⁶But a certain maid beheld him as he sat by the fire, and earnestly looked upon him, and said, 'This man was also with Him.' ⁵⁷And he denied Him, saying, 'Woman, I know Him not.' " (Luke 22:56-57)

The consequences to Peter, if he had admitted being with Jesus, are unknown. They might have taken him and put him on trial, too! We'll never know! He denied knowing Jesus! Strike one!

Denial #2

"And after a little while another saw him, and said, 'Thou art also of them.' And Peter said, 'Man, I am not.' " (Luke 22:58)

Strike two!

Denial #3

"⁵⁹And about the space of one hour after another confidently affirmed, saying, 'Of a truth this fellow also was with Him: for he is a Galilaean.'

⁶⁰And Peter said, 'Man, I know not what thou sayest.' And immediately, while he yet spoke, the cock crew.

[61]"**And the Lord turned and looked upon Peter. . . .**" (Luke 22:59-61)

Jesus was correct! Peter was wrong! Strike three! OUT!

What was Peter's reaction? "**And Peter went out, and wept bitterly.**" (Luke 22:62)

Peter knew that the Lord Jesus was correct — that he (Peter) was a lot weaker than he thought! . . . and he had a lot to learn about himself!

Peter did learn! . . . and after the day of Pentecost, when Peter received the indwelling Holy Spirit, he lived a long life of great service to the Lord Jesus Christ! . . . and it was a life of fellowship with the Lord as well!

God had gained a son in the person of Peter, with whom He would enjoy many years of fellowship!

The End of Peter's Life

After Jesus' resurrection, He came unto His disciples and prepared a meal for them. After that meal, Jesus had a conversation with Peter. He asked Peter three times whether or not Peter loved Him. Surely, this reminded Peter of the three times he denied the Lord. . . . but then, Jesus said the following to Peter:

"[18]'**Verily, verily, I say unto thee, When thou wast young, thou girdest thyself, and walkedst whither thou wouldest: but when thou shalt be old, thou shalt stretch forth thy hands, and another shall gird thee, and carry thee whither thou wouldest not.'**

[19]**This spake he, signifying by what death he should glorify God. And when he had spoken this, he saith unto him, 'Follow Me.'** " (John 21:18-19)

Jesus told Peter that he would live a long life, but then, he would be taken prisoner and he would be crucified!

Peter lived his whole life from that day forward with the thought in mind that he was going to be crucified at the end of his life. Can you imagine going through life knowing for a certainty that you will one day be crucified? That is the burden Peter carried with him all the rest of his life!

This might even have helped Peter's boldness from that day forward! If you know death is relatively far off, and you know death by crucifixion is certain, and you know that the Holy Spirit is with you, you can and should dare to be bold in your service to the Lord! . . . and Peter was bold!

Each of us needs to take this into consideration for our own lives!

Peter's Life When Indwelt by the Holy Spirit

About 50 days after Jesus spoke to Peter, the Holy Spirit was given to all believers. How did Peter handle himself under the power of the Holy Spirit?

As we noted, Peter was always quick to speak, but before he was indwelt by the Holy Spirit, when he found himself in a spot, he failed. He claimed he would die for the Lord, but when accused of being one of the Lord's followers, he denied knowing the Lord.

After Peter was indwelt by the Holy Spirit, however, he was still quick to speak, but his hesitation to admit knowing the Lord disappeared.

In Acts 3:6, Peter and John healed a lame man by the power of the Lord: **"Then Peter said, "Silver and gold have I none; but such as I have give I thee: In the name of Jesus Christ of Nazareth rise up and walk."**

When the people gathered to hear what Peter had to say, Luke recorded the following words from Peter:

"[13]The God of Abraham, and of Isaac, and of Jacob, the God of our fathers, hath glorified His Son Jesus; whom ye delivered up, and denied Him in the presence of Pilate, when he was determined to let Him go. [14]But ye denied the Holy One and the Just, and desired a murderer to be granted unto you; [15]and killed the Prince of life, whom God hath raised from the dead; whereof we are witnesses. [16]And His name through faith in His name hath made this man strong, whom ye see and know: yea, the faith which is by Him hath given him this perfect soundness in the presence of you all." (Acts 3:13-16)

Does that sound like a man who feared for his life from this crowd he was addressing? No! Peter spoke out similarly on behalf of the Lord Jesus Christ throughout the rest of his life! He declared that the people had **"denied the Holy One and the Just,"** and that they had **"killed the Prince of life."** Those are mighty bold words! Stephen was stoned for similar words!

Consider the next chapter also.

"[1]And as they spake unto the people, the priests, and the captain of the temple, and the Sadducees, came upon them, [2]being grieved that

they taught the people, and preached through Jesus the resurrection from the dead." (Acts 4:1-2)

Here, you see that the religious leaders were "**grieved**" by the teaching and preaching of Peter and John. What did Peter say on this occasion to the religious leaders?

"[8]Then Peter, filled with the Holy Ghost, said unto them, 'Ye rulers of the people, and elders of Israel, [9]if we this day be examined of the good deed done to the impotent man, by what means he is made whole; [10]be it known unto you all, and to all the people of Israel, that by the name of Jesus Christ of Nazareth, whom ye crucified, whom God raised from the dead, even by Him doth this man stand here before you whole.

[11]This is the stone which was set at nought of you builders, which is become the head of the corner.

[12]Neither is there salvation in any other: for there is none other name under heaven given among men, whereby we must be saved.' " (Acts 4:8-12)

Here, Peter addressed "**the rulers of the people, and the elders of Israel.**" (vs 8) Again, he rightly accused that they had "**crucified**" "**Jesus Christ of Nazareth.**" He also declared that there is "**none other name under heaven**" "**whereby we must be saved.**"

Peter was indwelt by the Holy Spirit who gives power, boldness, and the right words for any occasion! Peter had no reason to hold back and every reason to speak up and tell the religious leaders and the people the whole truth of God! . . . and he did so — boldly! No more hanging back or denying the Lord!

Surely, the Lord God is enjoying the fellowship of men like Peter who are children of God and members of Jesus' generation!

The Lord God is moving closer and closer to having His heart's desire: a family of His own with whom He can fellowship throughout eternity!

38

God's Likeness Recovered

We started this study by noting that Adam was created in **the image and likeness of God**. But then, when Adam sinned, **he lost both** that image and that likeness. Following his sin, God kicked Adam and Eve out of the garden! Then in Genesis 5:3, we read that Seth, child of Adam and Eve, was born in **Adam's image and likeness — not God's**.

Let's look further at this word *likeness*. The word *likeness* means "*resemblance*, concretely *model, shape*." (Strong's) According to Vine, it means "likeness; shape; figure; form; pattern." (Vine, p 136)

Vine says that the Hebrew word for *likeness*, which is $d^e m \hat{u} t$ "signifies the original after which a thing is patterned." (Vine, p 137) Vine also declared this to be the sense of the use of the word in Genesis 1:26.

The Likeness of Adam

The pattern of God, after which Adam was formed, was without sin, but with free will. No one has ever seen God, so we can't say that Adam looked like God, but he was like God in all important ways. All external and internal features of Adam's form — arms, legs, hands, feet, body, head, brain, heart, eyes, ears, nose, mouth, etc. — and all of his non-physical attributes such as soul, spirit, free will, ability to reason, speak, love, joy, sorrow, etc. — correspond to attributes of God. God, who is a Spirit, may not physically look like Adam, but each ability we can list for Adam corresponds to an important ability of God.

For example, man has a nose and the ability to smell. After the flood, Noah offered burnt offerings of the clean beasts and clean fowl on the ark. Then, we read, "**And the LORD smelled a sweet savour . . .**" (Genesis 8:21) We can take each ability, attribute, feature, and function of man and relate it to God's abilities in similar fashion.

God made man with the ability to chose and act as an independent being. We call this *free will*. The potential to go astray in a direction different from the wishes of God was inherent in man.

Sure enough, at his first opportunity, Adam chose to disobey God. When he took a bite of the fruit of the tree of the knowledge of good and evil, the **likeness** of man to God was **lost!** Adam's spirit died to God immediately and his body began its slow downward spiral towards physical death!

Seth was born to Adam and Eve, as recorded in Genesis 5:3. **"And Adam lived an hundred and thirty years, and begat a son in his own likeness, after his image; and called his name Seth."**

Notice the distinction Moses made here with the birth of Seth. Moses declared that Seth was born in the **likeness** of **Adam**, his fallen, sinful father. Moses had no need to make this distinction if Seth still maintained the complete likeness to God. . . . but with Adam's sin nature, he and all of his children were no longer like God!

Note that neither of the two character traits, *sinful* nor *disobedient*, apply to God. Throughout eternity, the Son of God never did anything but that which the Father desired. The Godhead did not know sin. They were familiar with the concept because Satan, and many angels with him, rebelled against God's leadership. But sin had no part in the Godhead! God made Adam without sin — but with free will!

Having given Adam free will, the possibility to sin existed. God knew this! He also knew that man needed to be free to choose! . . . and God knew man would choose to disobey.

Because God knew man would disobey and sin would enter this world, God determined the plan of salvation before the foundation of the world!

The Man Jesus

The Son of God, who was with God throughout eternity, was **given** to man by God. The Son of God, who was **born** as a man in a stable to Mary, was known to us as Jesus.

Jesus' mother was Mary; Jesus' Father was God! As such, Jesus was fully human, and fully God! As a human child of Mary, he looked exactly like any other man! . . . but as the Son of God, He was totally separate from sin! Plus, Jesus' Spirit was always alive to God! . . . unlike Adam's spirit which was dead to God!

Externally, Jesus took the physical pattern of a man. Internally, Jesus enjoyed all the great and wonderful attributes of God! . . . and throughout His whole life on earth, Jesus was in constant communication with God the Father!

Believers

Man's Original State

Every believer in this world started life as a descendant of Adam. Every child throughout history has been born in Adam's sinful likeness — both externally and internally — which means each of us has been born with indwelling sin.

The State of Believers

When a believer, in faith, turns his/her life over to Jesus Christ, He gives them eternal life. This also means that one day, all who believe will receive new resurrection bodies in which we will spend eternity in the presence of both the Lord Jesus Christ and God the Father!

What do we learn about the **likeness** of believers who are members of the family of God?

This is an important point! This following verse gives the Apostle John's explanation:

"**Beloved, now are we the sons of God, and it doth not yet appear what we shall be: but we know that, when He shall appear, <u>we shall be like Him</u>; for we shall see Him as He is.**" (1 John 3:2)

When Jesus gathers all believers together, we shall see Him as He is, and "<u>we shall be like Him</u>."

For all believers during eternity, our bodies and our minds will be like His! That which Adam lost, believers will regain!

Adam lost the **likeness** of God when he sinned, but when believers are gathered to the Lord in the next life, we will regain the **likeness of**

God! Believers, in this life, are already free from sin. "**But now being made free from sin, and become servants to God, ye have your fruit unto holiness, and the end everlasting life.**" (Romans 6:22)

The spirits of all believers in this life have been quickened and are alive to God, but since we still dwell in fallen bodies, there is constant conflict. Actions which originate from our bodies, independent of guidance from God, are sinful. Actions which originate from our spirits, guided by the Holy Spirit of God, are without sin. These two driving forces battle constantly within believers until the day we die. Only after death will we ever be free from these fallen bodies. Resurrection bodies which we will receive at the Lord's return will be totally perfect and without sin.

Until that time, however, believers will fight an internal battle with sin throughout this lifetime in these mortal bodies. To the extent which we allow the Holy Spirit to guide our spirits to follow God's desires, we can behave without sin. To the extent which we allow our fallen bodies to reign in our lives, we will continue to sin. Such is the battle!

Resurrection Bodies

When we are completely **like** Jesus Christ in that day, we will be in resurrection bodies! What do we know about resurrection bodies? Paul talked about them in 1 Corinthians 15.

"**[42]So also is the resurrection of the dead.**

It is sown in corruption;

> **It is raised in incorruption:**

[43]It is sown in dishonour;

> **It is raised in glory:**

It is sown in weakness;

> **It is raised in power:**

[44]It is sown a natural body;

> **It is raised a spiritual body:**

There is a natural body,

> **And there is a spiritual body.**" (1 Corinthians 15:42-44)

Mankind's natural bodies are **corruptible**. Without physical life, flesh decays — it corrupts.   . . . but our resurrection bodies will be **incorruptible**.

Natural bodies are **dishonorable**, being inhabited by all manner of evil lusts and desires, but resurrection bodies will be **raised in glory** with no negative qualities at all!

Natural bodies are **weak**! Look at anyone who has a debilitating illness and that will show you how weak these bodies truly are! . . . but resurrection bodies will be **raised in power**. They will not be susceptible to human weakness.

Natural bodies are not spiritual because Adam's spirit died the instant he bit into the forbidden fruit! . . . but resurrection bodies will be **spiritual bodies** – completely alive to God!

Do we know exactly what our resurrection bodies will be like? No! That was what John was saying in 1 John 3:2. We don't know exactly what we will be like. Our human limitations don't let us completely fathom the abilities and character of resurrection bodies! . . . but we do know this: when we receive resurrection bodies, they will be **like** Jesus' resurrection body! . . . and that will be totally marvelous!

Every believer is awaiting the change of his/her mortal body to a resurrection body on the day when the Lord returns to gather His own! (Romans 8:11, 1 Corinthians 15:52) The souls of those who die before the Lord returns go directly to be with Him in paradise (Luke 23:43), as did the soul of the repentant thief at the crucifixion. All souls in paradise are also awaiting their resurrection bodies – which they also will receive on the day Jesus returns to earth!

What About Our Hearts and Minds?

For this, we need to consider **renewal**. Renewing of believers' hearts starts the day we receive the Holy Spirit.

"Not by works of righteousness which we have done, but according to His mercy He saved us, by the washing of regeneration, and renewing of the Holy Ghost." (Titus 3:5)

The day we are saved, our spirits, which were dead compliments of Adam's sin, are brought to life (quickened) by God! That same instant, the Holy Spirit enters, takes residence in our hearts, and starts the **renewal** process.

Those who put their faith in the Lord Jesus Christ **have** everlasting life. (John 3:16) Paul wrote that God "<u>hath</u> **quickened us together with Christ.**" (Ephesians 2:5) He also wrote, **"And you <u>hath</u> He quickened .**

. . ." (Ephesians 2:1) God has **already** quickened the spirits of all believers in Christ.

Spiritual quickening, that is, newness of life, occurs **instantly** upon salvation! It is not something for which we must wait a specified period of time. Paul added:

"¹⁰**And if Christ be in you, the body is dead because of sin; but** the Spirit is life **because of righteousness.** ¹¹**But if the Spirit of Him that raised up Jesus from the dead dwell in you, He that raised up Christ from the dead shall also quicken your mortal bodies by His Spirit that dwelleth in you.**" (Romans 8:10-11)

Spiritual growth occurs throughout this life from the moment of our salvation forward! All believers are being molded to be **like** the Lord from the day we are saved. . . . and we become more and more **like** Him as we mature in His ways.

This author's mother-in-law had a framed calligraphy on her kitchen wall which said: "PBPWMGNFWMY." This meant, "Please be patient with me — God's not finished with me yet!" The renewal and maturation processes of believers are gradual — only ending at death. But then, instantly, our **likeness** to the Lord will be total and complete!

As we go through our lives as Christians, the Holy Spirit has time to mould us to be **like** the Son of God!

"**For we which live are alway delivered unto death for Jesus' sake, that the life also of Jesus might be made manifest in our mortal flesh.**" (2 Corinthians 4:11)

Believers who are alive in this world, can begin to show the life of Jesus in their mortal flesh. The power of that life is even more evident when a believer, like Stephen, is being delivered unto death, or when a believer is being severely stressed!

Spiritual life begins instantly upon salvation, and spiritual growth occurs throughout the remainder of a believer's life on earth. We grow spiritually throughout our walk on earth with Jesus Christ. Ultimately, when we stand in our resurrection bodies together with Him, we will be 100% **like** Him!

Summary

Adam was made in **God's likeness,** but he **lost** that likeness when he disobeyed God. Every one of Adam's descendants was born in **Adam's likeness** — the likeness of sinful man!

When God sent Jesus among us, He was born of Mary. He was a man, just like the rest of us. But Jesus' Father was God, not Adam. So Jesus was **not** born in the likeness of sinful man. Jesus, Son of God, was born a man! . . . yet He walked this earth as God — completely without sin!

When a man, woman, or child, puts his/her faith in the Son of God Jesus Christ, he/she instantly receives spiritual life which is eternal. That also sets each believer on a path towards life eternal in the presence of both God the Father and Jesus Christ the Son.

Once started on that pathway to heaven, it means that on the day of Jesus' return (His second coming), each person's body will be resurrected and reunited with both spirit and soul. When Jesus returns for His people, all believers will be given resurrection bodies, and we will then be **completely like Him!**

Those who reject God will go to the grave in the likeness of sinful Adam! . . . and they will remain separate from God forever! Those who reject God will receive their wish — they will not have to spend a single day in His presence!

Regarding the issue of the **likeness** of God, this is the sum: Adam, who was created in the **likeness of God,** sinned — and **lost** that **likeness!** All mankind begin life in the **likeness of sinful Adam!** Believers in Jesus Christ look forward to eternity future, when they will completely **regain** the **likeness of God** — that is, the **likeness of Jesus Christ!**

39

God's Image Recovered

God's Image Lost

We also started this study showing that man was made in the **image of God!** (Genesis 1:26)

The word *image* means "a representative *figure*, especially an *idol*." (Strong's) We understand that the word *image* carries with it the thought of representation. Being made in the image of God, Adam was to be God's representative on earth.

But once again, when Adam sinned, he **lost** the image of God.

In Genesis 5:3, when Seth was born, he was born **in the image and likeness of Adam**. He looked like Adam and he represented Adam. Every one of Adam's descendants has been born like Seth — in Adam's image and likeness.

Of whom are we all representative? . . . fallen Adam! We were all meant to be representatives of God, but that did not happen.

God's Image Regained

We already showed that we were born **like** sinful Adam, but all those who put their faith in Jesus Christ will one day be **like Him!**

Likeness lost! Likeness regained!

With regard to the image of God, is there a parallel? Yes!

"²⁸**And we know that all things work together for good to them that love God, to them who are the called according to His purpose.**

²⁹For whom He did foreknow, He also did predestinate to be conformed to the image of His Son, that He might be the firstborn among many brethren." (Romans 8:28-29)

"⁹Lie not one to another, seeing that ye have put off the old man with his deeds; ¹⁰and have put on the new man, which is renewed in knowledge after the image of Him that created Him." (Colossians 3:9-10)

God, who is omniscient, knows all! . . . and He knows who will and who will not accept His mercy and grace. All those who accept God's offer of salvation, according to verse 29, "**He also did predestinate to be conformed to the image of His Son.**"

Adam was God's representative on earth, but he lost that image when he sinned. Jesus came to earth as God's representative, and He retains that image always!

We, who are the Lord's people, **will all be conformed to the image of His Son,** which is the very image of God! Where does it say that? Jesus, the Son, is "**the express image of His person.**" (Hebrews 1:3) The word "**His**" in this verse refers directly to "**God.**" (Hebrews 1:1) Jesus is the express image of God's Person!

So all believers will be conformed to the image of the Son, who is the express image of God the Father! This explains the growth which occurs in a believer from the day of their salvation forward. The Holy Spirit works in this life to mould each believer into the image of the Son of God. In believers, this is an ever-present work-in-progress!

But when Jesus returns for us, and gives us our resurrection bodies, that work of conformation will instantly be complete! We will then be in **His image**!

Image lost! Image regained!

Believers will go throughout eternity bearing the **image** and **likeness** of God! We lost both for a time in this life, but we will regain both for all eternity!

We will again be **like** Jesus, and we will be His representatives (in His **image**) throughout eternity!

40

A Brand New Start
Where All Is Perfect!

Now let's look at the description the Bible gives of eternity future! It will be a wonderful place in which all believers who ever lived will dwell and bask in the presences of God the Father, Jesus Christ the Son, and the Holy Spirit.

Who Will Be There?

From God's Point-of-View

The people who will be with God throughout eternity will include all of God's children of all ages from earth. All, like Abraham, who believed God, will be there! All, who put their faith in the Lord Jesus Christ throughout this life, who want to be with Him throughout eternity, who want to love Him, who want to fellowship with Him, and who want to be His people, will be there!

All whose names are **"written in the Lamb's book of life,"** (Revelation 21:27) will be there! All those who **"do His commandments, that they have right to the tree of life,"** will **"enter in through the gates into the city."** (Revelation 22:14) All of the Lord's people will be there!

As we said at the beginning of this study, God wants a people of His own whom He can love, for whom He can care, with whom He can fellowship, and whose company He can enjoy. God will have all of His beloved people with Him throughout eternity!

From Man's Point-of-View

New Testament Saints

- All of those people, who put their trust and faith in the Lord Jesus Christ throughout the New Testament era (Paul, Stephen, Peter, and all Christians), will be there.

Old Testament Believers

- All of those people of the Old Testament era, who believed God (like Abraham did), will be there.

Miscarried & Aborted Babies

- All miscarried and aborted babies, who never had the chance to experience life outside their mothers' wombs, will be there! Life begins at conception, and all of those innumerable souls will be there!

Children

- All children who died before they matured enough to understand they had the choice to believe, or not believe, the Lord, will be there!

We know this about children because when the young child of David and Bathsheba died, David said, **"But now he is dead, wherefore should I fast? can I bring him back again? I shall go to him, but he shall not return to me."** (2 Samuel 12:23)

We know David was a man of God. We know that upon his death, he went straight to heaven to be with the Lord! In heaven, David fully expected to see his child again! **"I shall go to him."** This statement by David should be great comfort to all parents who have lost a young child!

My sister died when she was a week old. My parents were not familiar with this verse, and the question regarding what would happen to their daughter after death was of great concern to them! They focused on, and were anxious about, this question for the whole week of her life. Surely, that anxiety carried on within them for years following. Had they known these words of David that their baby girl would go directly to heaven, they would have been greatly comforted!

What Will Heaven Be Like?

The last two chapters of the Bible speak of heaven and eternity. First, we read John's reassuring statement which shows God's purpose for mankind: **"the tabernacle of God is with men, and He will dwell with them, and they shall be His people, and God Himself shall be with them, and be their God."** (Revelation 21:3)

This statement is almost identical to the promise God made to the children of Israel in the Old Testament. . . . and here it is again at the end of the Bible, where it reaffirms God's desire towards mankind!

Everyone in this life awaits the day of their death. Many are extremely nervous about that day! Some greatly fear death! . . . but to the Lord's children, to know that God is looking forward to spending eternity with them is a very comforting thought!

What Will NOT Be There?

Next, John goes on to describe life in heaven:

"And God shall wipe away all tears from their eyes; and there shall be no more death, neither sorrow, nor crying, neither shall there be any more pain: for the former things are passed away." (Revelation 21:4)

There are several **no more**'s which will characterize the city of New Jerusalem of eternity future:

"And I saw no temple therein: for the Lord God Almighty and the Lamb are the temple of it." (Revelation 21:22)

"And the city had no need of the sun, neither of the moon, to shine in it: for the glory of God did lighten it, and the Lamb is the light thereof." (Revelation 21:23)

"And the gates of it shall not be shut at all by day: for there shall be no night there." (Revelation 21:25)

"And there shall be no more curse: but the throne of God and of the Lamb shall be in it; and His servants shall serve Him." (Revelation 22:3)

"And there shall be no night there; and they need no candle, neither light of the sun; for the Lord God giveth them light: and they shall reign for ever and ever." (Revelation 22:5)

Now let's list everything which will **not** be present during eternity future:

- tears,
- sorrow,
- pain,
- curse,
- moon,
- candles, and
- death,
- crying,
- temple,
- sun,
- night,
- light of the sun.

Some of these are the very things which make life in this world terrible, which result from tribulations and afflictions to mankind! Tears, death, sorrow, crying, pain, etc., will **not** tarnish eternity!

Some of these, like the sun and the moon, will no longer be needed — being replaced by the glory of the Lamb, who will be the lamp throughout eternity!   . . . and with the Lamb supplying the light throughout eternity, there will no longer be night, nor the need for any other source of light!

What and Who WILL Be There?

There will be many wonderful things, and many wonderful persons in heaven! Consider all of these verses:

"And He said unto me, 'It is done. I am Alpha and Omega, the beginning and the end. I will give unto him that is athirst of the fountain of the water of life freely.' " (Revelation 21:6)

"He that overcometh shall inherit all things; and I will be his God, and he shall be My son." (Revelation 21:7)

"And the nations of them which are saved shall walk in the light of it: and the kings of the earth do bring their glory and honour into it." (Revelation 21:24)

"And they shall bring the glory and honour of the nations into it." (Revelation 21:26)

"And He shewed me a pure river of water of life, clear as crystal, proceeding out of the throne of God and of the Lamb." (Revelation 22:1)

"In the midst of the street of it, and on either side of the river, was there the tree of life, which bare twelve manner of fruits, and yielded her fruit every month: and the leaves of the tree were for the healing of the nations." (Revelation 22:2)

"And they shall see His [the Lamb's] face; and His name shall be in their foreheads." (Revelation 22:4)

"And, behold, I come quickly; and My reward is with Me, to give every man according as his work shall be." (Revelation 22:12)

In the throne room of God, we find:

"The four and twenty elders fall down before Him that sat on the throne, and worship Him that liveth for ever and ever, and cast their crowns before the throne." (Revelation 4:10)

"And I beheld, and I heard the voice of many angels round about the throne and the beasts and the elders: and the number of them was ten thousand times ten thousand, and thousands of thousands." (Revelation 5:11)

Now let's make a list of all which, and whom, we will find in heaven:

- the Lord God,
- the Holy Spirit,
- the visible Lamb's face,
- the 24 elders,
- all saints,
- our eternal inheritance,
- the honor of the nations,
- the river of the water of life,
- the tree of life, and
- the Lord's rewards to His people!

- the Son of God,
- God's angels,
- the Lamb's name,
- the living beings,
- the water of life,
- the glory of the nations,
- the nations of the saved,
- the glory of earth's kings,

Surely, this is an incomplete list, but the idea is clear: the heavenly city and eternity future will be a joyous place!

Note that there are **no** negatives in this list. Everything and everyone in heaven will be glorious! These are the reasons why we know heaven as *paradise!*

The Lord God and the Son have seen fit to make heaven the wonderful, glorious place, and the experience the likes of which we have never known!

Who Will NOT Be There?

There are quite a few individuals who will have no part in heaven, nor eternity future in the presence of God. Let's consider those verses:

"And the devil that deceived them was cast into the lake of fire and brimstone, where the beast and false prophet are, and shall be tormented day and night for ever and ever." (Revelation 20:10)

"And death and hell were cast into the lake of fire. This is the second death." (Revelation 20:14)

"And whosoever was not found written in the book of life was cast into the lake of fire." (Revelation 20:15)

"But the fearful, and unbelieving, and the abominable, and murderers, and whoremongers, and sorcerers, and idolaters, and all liars, shall have their part in the lake which burneth with fire and brimstone: which is the second death." (Revelation 21:8)

"And there shall in no wise enter into it any thing that defileth, neither whatsoever worketh abomination, or maketh a lie: but they which are written in the Lamb's book of life." (Revelation 21:27)

"For without are dogs, and sorcerers, and whoremongers, and murderers, and idolaters, and whosoever loveth and maketh a lie." (Revelation 22:15)

Note that John used the descriptor **"dogs,"** in Revelation 22:15, in its metaphorical sense. He wasn't talking about the family pet! The label *dog* is used throughout the Bible to describe people whose filthy, disgusting behavior is similar to what one can expect of the average dog. Such behavior should not characterize any man — but it often does.

Here is a list of those who will not be present in heaven throughout eternity:

- Satan, the devil,
- the false prophet,
- the fearful,
- abominations,
- whoremongers,
- idolaters,
- any**thing** that defileth,
- any**one** who maketh a lie,
- any**one** who worketh abomination, and
- all whose names are **not** found written in the book of life.
- the beast,
- death and hell,
- the unbelieving,
- murderers,
- sorcerers,
- liars,
- any**thing** that maketh a lie,
- filthy, disgusting men (dogs),

These are all the negatives — the evils and evil ones of this world. None of them will be present to mar, darken, nor even cast a shadow upon eternity!

Recognize that all of mankind who find themselves in this list had every chance, but still chose to reject the Lord God's every offer of forgiveness, salvation, and life!

While still in this life, no one who finds themselves on this list needs to remain on it! The Lord God will forgive all who humbly repent, put their faith in His Son Jesus Christ, ask His forgiveness, and trust Him! Until death closes the eyes of each person, it is never too late! But the instant death takes a person who has steadfastly refused, rejected, and denied the Lord, their future is set! . . . and they will remain on this list — forever!

Jesus Christ Will Be In Heaven

Of course, the Lord Jesus, who goes by many great and wonderful names, will be in heaven throughout eternity with all of His people. Here are the names by which He is known, and by which He will continue to be known! These names are from just the last four chapters of Revelation:

- Christ,
- Alpha and Omega,
- the beginning and the end,
- the first and the last,
- the Lamb,
- Faithful and True,
- the Word of God,
- the King of kings,
- the bright and morning star,
- the Lord of lords,
- the root of David, and
- the offspring of David.

All of these descriptors accurately characterize the Lord's many beautiful attributes! He will be in heaven! . . . and He will be with His beloved people throughout eternity! . . . and all believers will be there to celebrate His many magnificent beauties forever!

The Lord God Almighty Will Be There

Also, of course, Almighty God will be in heaven with His people. This has always been His desire — to live and dwell with a people of His own. He wants to be able to love them, care for them, and fellowship with them! In the heaven of eternity future, all of His desires will be fulfilled!

In these last chapters of Revelation, we see God referred to by several names as well. He is called:

- the Lord God omnipotent,
- the great God, and
- the Lord God Almighty,
- Almighty God.

All of these titles are perfectly accurate as they characterize the God of the universe!

All believers, who will be privileged to spend eternity with God and with His Son, will spend eternity learning all of the magnificent and wonderful details which led to these many great names by which the Father and the Son are known!

Eternity is a long time! . . . and it will take that long for us to fully appreciate and know the Lord God Almighty and His precious Son! . . . and all the while, we will all be enjoying wonderful fellowship together — with each other, with God Almighty, and with the Lord Jesus Christ!

41

Summary

We began this study with the following question: Why did God create man? The evidence points to the answer that God wants a people — a family — of His own whom He can love, with whom He can fellowship, and for whom He can care.

With that goal in mind, God created this world as a dwelling place for man, and then He created all manner of life — mankind, plants, and animals — to dwell therein also.

So let's review our study to see if all the evidence truly does point to this answer!

Adam and Eve

God created Adam in His own image and His own likeness. Adam was created like God to be God's representative on earth. Man's likeness to God allows fellowship between God and man. Then, recognizing that it was not good for man to dwell alone, God created Eve to be Adam's wife.

God also created a beautiful garden in which He placed **every** fruit-bearing tree. Included among the trees were the tree of the knowledge of good and evil, and the tree of life. Except for the fruit of the tree of the knowledge of good and evil, Adam and Eve could eat freely of any of the fruit in the garden, including the fruit of the tree of life. They were forbidden to eat fruit from only that **one** tree — the tree of the knowledge of good and evil.

For man to be created like God, man was given free will. He could choose freely what he did or didn't do, what he did or didn't say, what he did or didn't believe, etc.

When the choice of food includes **every** possible type of fruit found on earth, which represents enormous variety, not being allowed to eat of **one** fruit is simply a test. . . . and Adam failed the test!

When Adam and Eve ate of the forbidden fruit, sin entered the world, and death accompanied sin. Spiritual death was immediate; physical death happened after long lives. After Adam sinned, God kicked Adam and Eve out of the garden, so they had no further access to the tree of life.

God cursed the serpent (the devil) for enticing Eve to eat the forbidden fruit. He cursed the earth as a result of Adam's sin. Then He imposed punishments on both Adam and Eve. Where life in the garden would have been easy and pleasurable, life following Adam's sin would be laborious and demanding!

Seth

God formed Adam in His own image and likeness! When Adam sinned, he not only fell out of God's good graces, but he **lost** both the image and the likeness of God. Adam no longer represented God on earth, and with sin indwelling and God's likeness lost, fellowship between Adam and God was broken as well.

When Seth was born to Adam and Eve, Moses noted that Seth was born in **Adam's** image and likeness (not God's). Seth, being born in the **image** of Adam, was a representative of his father Adam. Seth, being also born in the **likeness** of Adam, had sin indwelling his mortal body.

Adam and Eve had other sons and daughters, who were similarly born in Adam's image and likeness. Down through the years, descendants of fallen Adam and Eve populated the earth.

Of all these people, it was difficult for God to find many with whom He could fellowship.

Noah

By Noah's day, which was several generations removed from Adam and Eve, the men and women of the earth had become desperately wicked!

God had had enough! He decided to destroy all life on the earth with a great flood! He intended to start over again. This time, He would reboot the earth, starting with Noah.

It turns out in the years before the great flood, that Noah was the **only** just man on the earth. Everyone else was terribly evil! We don't know anything about the character of the members of Noah's family. They were on the ark, not because they were just, but because they were Noah's family — and Noah was just!

God directed Noah to build an ark in which he, his wife, their three sons, and their wives, would survive the flood. In the ark, God also placed a pair of every type of animal. Following the flood, all varieties of life which God created on earth, which had been saved through the flood by the ark, could continue.

After the great flood, God told Noah and his family to replenish the earth! Each pair of animals was expected to reproduce and replenish the earth as well. This was a fresh start for the earth.

One of the first things Noah did after the flood, however, was to plant a vineyard, grow grapes, make wine, and get drunk. Noah, his wife and children, were all descendants of Adam and Eve which means they were all indwelt by sin. Although Noah was just, and he was obedient in the building of the ark, he demonstrated by getting drunk and dishonoring himself that he was still a descendant of Adam!

So as the earth began to be repopulated, the sin problem continued to increase and spread, and the mores of society once again continued their downward slide. Just as Adam's descendants failed to produce a people God could call His own and with whom God could fellowship, Noah's descendants were following that same downward path.

Abraham

Some generations later, God approached Abraham and told him to depart to a new land. God promised to give Abraham and his descendants the land of Canaan for ever.

This was not a completely new start like God had done with Adam nor with Noah. God chose Abraham, out of all mankind, to be the father of a family the Lord intended to be His own!

The trait which distinguished Abraham from everyone else was that **he believed God**, and for that **faith**, God credited him with righteousness! (Note: to believe = to have faith.) God made great and wonderful promises to Abraham and to his descendants: God promised to bless Abraham's family, and to bless all the nations of the world through one of Abraham's descendants.

Isaac

Isaac was the son God promised to Abraham and his wife Sarah. All of the promises God had made to Abraham, were confirmed to Isaac.

Jacob/Israel

Isaac had two sons, Esau and Jacob. Unto Jacob, God confirmed the promises He had made to Abraham and to Isaac. So Jacob, who would later be renamed Israel, became the father of the line of people whom God called His own!

Jacob had twelve sons, each of whom became the head of a large family. The twelve families became known as **the twelve tribes of Israel**, and the whole family became known as **the children of Israel**.

The Children of Israel

The families of Jacob's twelve sons were God's chosen people. God planned for them to fellowship with Him, love Him, and obey His commandments. In return, He would be their God; He would love them; He would care for them: and He would guide them throughout their lives.

When the children of Israel became slaves in the land of Egypt, God sent Moses and Aaron to rescue them. The message to Pharaoh from the Lord was, "**Let My people go.**" Moses repeated these precise words many times to Pharaoh to clearly show God's relationship to the children of Israel.

After rescuing the children of Israel from Egypt, and all the while they were wandering in the wilderness of Sinai, the children of Israel did little but complain and rebel against God's leadership. As descendants of Adam, they demonstrated over and over again that they all had the indwelling sin problem! . . . and with their free will, they chose to reject the Lord rather than listen to Him.

Joshua

At God's command, Moses rescued the people from Egypt and led them into the wilderness of Sinai. But when the Lord wanted the people to enter the promised land, they refused. Why? . . . because they were afraid of the people of the land.

For refusing God's guidance to enter the land immediately, He made them wander in the desert until all adults who were rescued from Egypt died. This took 40 years. The only two men who came out of Egypt, who entered the promised land, were Joshua and Caleb. Both of them were among the twelve who scouted the land of Canaan about two years after their rescue from Egypt. Both wanted to obey the Lord and enter the land immediately. But the other ten scouts and all the people refused to enter the land at that time. Therefore, God forced them to spend another 38 years wandering in the wilderness.

After 40 years in the wilderness, and after the death of Moses, when the people were again poised to enter the land, the Lord put Joshua in charge.

Joshua led the people across the Jordan river into the promised land, and he led them as they conquered the land promised to them by God.

Having taken the land, Joshua distributed the Lord's inheritances (parcels of the land of Canaan) to the people.

But the children of Israel hadn't driven out nor destroyed all of the peoples of the land as God directed! As a result, many evil influences had come among the children of Israel. These included all types of idols, heathen gods, and worship practices of the peoples of the land.

The children of Israel continued to sin and fall further and further away from the Lord God. Then, they actually began to worship the idols and heathen gods — all practices which were abomination to the Lord!

Very few of the children of Israel wanted to be children of the Lord God!

Judges

After the death of Joshua, the Lord began to appoint judges (leaders) to rule the people. About that time, a cycle began to appear.

The people would reject the Lord, which would kindle His anger against them. He would then deliver the people into the hands of an enemy. Instead of having a peaceful life in the promised land, they found themselves captives and slaves to enemy kings. When they were sufficiently upset about their slavery, and they cried to the Lord for help, He would establish a new judge to rescue them and rule over them.

Under the leadership of the new judge, the people would again return to the land to lead peaceful lives and worship God. . . . but when the judge died, the people would immediately revert back to their heathen gods, and reject the Lord God of Israel anew.

This cycle, which described the relationship of the people to the Lord God, was up, down, up, down, etc.

The cycle continued through several judges. Towards the end of the time of the judges, we read a terrible statement:

"In those days there was no king in Israel: every man did that which was right in his own eyes." (Judges 21:25)

The Lord God was guiding Israel! The children of Israel were totally ignoring Him — even though He was functioning as their king! They were doing anything and everything they felt like doing! They preferred anarchy and all of its inherent societal problems, to the peace and quiet they could have enjoyed under the Lord's leadership. They rejected the Lord God of Israel! . . . and called for a king! . . . a human king!

Kings of Israel and Judah

The children of Israel enjoyed a unique situation. The Lord God of the universe wanted to be their God! He wanted to lead them, love them, care for them, fellowship with them, etc. But they ignored Him and rejected His every offer!

Instead, they wanted a king! All the nations around them had kings! . . . and they wanted a king, too! God suggested they didn't understand their request, so He had Samuel warn them about kings. Even after the warning, they insisted they wanted a king!

God then told Samuel that He recognized their desire for a king as the rejection, not of Samuel, but of Himself! They were rejecting the Lord God! . . . so God gave them a king!

Saul

The Lord chose Saul to be their first king. Whereas Saul was quite humble when he was a nobody, after he became king, he began to think highly of himself! . . . and this led him to ignore the Lord God and do as he pleased! So God took the kingdom away from him and gave it to David.

David

King David was a man after God's own heart. (Acts 13:22) All his life, David did "**that which was right in the eyes of the Lord.**" David walked with God, except . . . "**save only in the matter of Uriah the Hittite.**" (1 Kings 15:5) Regarding Uriah, David sinned in a huge way!

David walked with the Lord all of his days! On that one occasion, however, David broke his fellowship with the Lord by causing Uriah's wife Bathsheba to conceive, and then ordering her husband Uriah killed in battle. That was a pretty major series of sins!

Other than that one incident, king David walked with God! That is, king David enjoyed fellowship with God throughout his life!

Solomon

Solomon, second son of David and Bathsheba, was loved by the Lord. The Lord went so far as to say about Solomon: "**I will be his father, and he shall be My son.**" (2 Samuel 7:14)

When Solomon became king, the Lord gifted him with great wisdom and riches. But as wise as Solomon was, in his old age, he sinned against the Lord by bringing heathen idols and worship practices among the children of Israel!

Hezekiah

Several kings later in the line of David and Solomon, Hezekiah became king of Judah. He was a great king who relied heavily on the counsel of God! God enjoyed fellowship with king Hezekiah.

Manasseh

Although Hezekiah was a great king, his son Manasseh was an evil king. The apple did not at all resemble the tree from which it fell.

Everything Hezekiah did that was good, which fostered fellowship with God, Manasseh did the opposite. Manasseh was a terrible king.

Josiah

Manasseh's grandson, Josiah, was another good king. . . . but Manasseh's son and Josiah's sons were evil like Manasseh.

When the Lord finally had enough, He handed over the people of Israel to the Assyrians, and He handed over the people of Judah to the Babylonians.

All of the children of Israel were then slaves in foreign lands, remaining there for seventy years.

The Son of God, Jesus, Comes to Earth

Now we jump ahead several hundred years. Having been totally rejected by the children of Israel, God gave His Son to be born a man, so He could live, walk, and talk among the people of earth! Jesus, who was the Son of the Almighty God of heaven, was born as a human baby unto Mary!

Jesus was 100% man and 100% God. He did not inherit indwelling sin from Adam, because God was His Father! As a child of Mary, however, He experienced life on earth as a man!

Jesus was the man, who would represent God and speak for God on earth. Jesus was the Prophet whom God promised to send to the children of Israel. (Deuteronomy 18:15-16)

Jesus was born in Bethlehem a descendant of king David. He was the One through whom God established the house of David for ever.

The people of Israel, however, rejected Him! They crucified Him! . . . but God raised Him from the dead! Jesus had no sin in Him, so death had no claim on Him!

Herein lies the solution to mankind's sin problem! When Jesus was crucified, He suffered at God's hands all punishments deserved for all sins of all mankind! Jesus paid all penalties on our behalf so we need not pay them ourselves! Since Jesus was totally free of sin, His suffering for sins was for **all of our** sins!

Now, God can forgive men, women, and children for their sins because all penalties for those sins have been paid-in-full by Jesus on the cross of Calvary. God's righteous requirements are intact and satisfied, because all sins have been punished, and all penalties paid!

God does not welcome anyone into His presence by just ignoring sins. That would be wrong! . . . but since all punishments for sins have been paid by Jesus Christ, God can forgive all of those who put their faith in Him! Then, having forgiven them, He can welcome them into His family!

Throughout the Old Testament, natural mankind went down, down, downhill into depravity until reaching rock bottom! That descent took the children of Israel further and further away from God!

When they finally reached the lowest possible level in the pit of depravity, Jesus came to earth to lift everyone out of that pit!

Practically speaking for life in these bodies, no one becomes perfect on the day of their salvation. We all fight with the flesh throughout our natural lives. Spiritually speaking, however, everyone comes alive to God on the day of their salvation. Our spirits, which were dead (compliments of Adam's sin) immediately become alive — quickened by Christ! The new life, which the Lord gives us at the instant of salvation, is eternal life! . . . and with the help of the Holy Spirit, who takes up residence in our hearts at the instant of salvation, we can learn and grow to be like Jesus!

The ascent of mankind out of depravity has been made possible by the selfless sacrifice of the Son of God, and by the power of the Holy Spirit of God!

Paul

Paul was a believer in Jesus Christ who was originally known as Saul. Saul was a Pharisee, a highly educated Jew, who was an enemy of both Jesus Christ and all Christians! He oversaw the stoning death of Stephen, and he captured, mistreated, and imprisoned many Christians!

But one day, Jesus Christ confronted him! All of his prior education and understanding came into proper focus instantly! From that day when he put his faith and trust in the Lord Jesus Christ, and for the rest of his earthly life, he faithfully served the Lord!

Before he was saved, Saul was a dynamic, harsh, evil man who hated Jesus Christ and all of His followers. After he was saved, Paul was a dynamic, brash, quickened man who loved the Lord and all of His followers! He put the earlier negative gusto with which he pursued and punished believers, into positive gusto with which he served the Lord, taught believers, and preached the Gospel to non-believers!

Stephen

Stephen was another New Testament believer in the Lord Jesus Christ. We know little about Stephen's early background, but as a Christian, he was full of the Holy Spirit as he served the Lord! . . . and when he was put on trial, he spoke fearlessly before the religious leaders of his day! . . . when he rebuked them for their behaviors and for their lack of faith in the Lord God, they put him to death!

During that brutal scene, we are told that his countenance looked like that of an angel, and he prayed with his last dying breath for the Lord to forgive his murderers! What a testimony!!!

Jesus stood up from His throne in heaven to welcome Stephen into the presence of God! What an example of a Spirit-filled believer Stephen showed us!

Peter

A third example of a believer in the Lord Jesus Christ, was Peter — one of the twelve Apostles. Before he was saved, Peter spoke quickly and thought later. He also thought he was really tough, and he could stand with the Lord Jesus — even unto death. But when that theory was put to the test, Peter failed!

As a Christian indwelt by the Holy Spirit of God, however, Peter stood up for the Lord and told everyone all that he feared to tell them in his earlier days when he did not have the help of the Holy Spirit! He correctly declared to their faces that the religious leaders of the Jews had crucified the Lord God! His hesitation to speak boldly was a thing of the past!

We also know that after His resurrection, Jesus told Peter that he would lead a long life and die by crucifixion. Peter went through his whole life of service to the Lord God knowing that one day, he would die by the same terrible method Jesus had suffered!

Peter was a bold, fearless Christian throughout his life which lasted many years!

The Likeness of God

Although Adam was made in the likeness of God, **he lost that likeness** when he sinned. But through the work of Jesus Christ, **all who believe will regain His likeness** when we stand in His presence!

"But we know that, when He shall appear, we shall be <u>like</u> Him." (1 John 3:2)

The Image of God

Likewise, Adam, who was made in the image of God, **lost that image** when he sinned. He no longer represented God on earth!

But again, through Jesus' sacrifice, death, and resurrection, **we will once again regain His image:**

"For whom He did foreknow, He also did predestinate to be conformed to the <u>image</u> of His Son . . ." (Romans 8:29)

Heaven and Eternity

Through Jesus' efforts, God's plans will be fulfilled! Eternity future will be occupied by all believers who want to spend it in God's presence, who want to be children of God, who want to love Him, who want to be loved by Him, and who want to enjoy fellowship with Him!

When we stand in His presence, we will be standing there in resurrection bodies which will be made in **the image and likeness of God!**

. . . and the Lord God's great desire will be fulfilled! He will be surrounded by a family of His own, all of whom chose to spend eternity with Him so they can enjoy His presence, the presence of His Son Jesus Christ, and eternal fellowship with God!

God bless all who will enjoy sweet fellowship with Him throughout eternity!

References

1. Vine's Complete Expository Dictionary of Old and New Testament Words, Thomas Nelson Publishers, Vine, W. E., Unger, Merrill F., and White, William Jr., Nashville, TN, 1985.
2. Strong, James, A Concise Dictionary of the Words in The Greek Testament; with their renderings in the Authorized English Version, Hendrickson Publishers, Peabody, MA.
3. Strong, James, A Concise Dictionary of the Words in The Hebrew Bible; with their renderings in the Authorized English Version, Hendrickson Publishers, Peabody, MA.
4. Webster's Seventh New Collegiate Dictionary, G. & C. Merriam Company, Springfield, MA, 1965.
5. Elpenor, http://www.ellopos.net/elpenor/default.asp.
6. Newberry, Thomas, "The Englishman's Bible," A Study Version of The Authorized Version, Penfold Book & Bible House, Bicester, England.
7. Clarke, Adam, "Commentary on the Bible," e-Sword, Version 7.9.8, 2008.

Books written by

Dennis R Dinger

are available at:

www.lulu.com   www.amazon.com

Christian Books include:

- Studies of Matthew, Mark, Luke, and John
- Studies of the Acts of the Apostles
- A Study of the Book of Romans
- Studies of Paul's Letters to the Corinthians
- GEPC — Studies of Galatians, Ephesians, Philippians, & Colossians
- Studies of Paul's Letters to the Thessalonians
- Studies of Paul's Letters to Timothy, Titus, & Philemon
- A Study of the Book of Hebrews
- A Study of the Letter of James
- Studies of the Letters of Peter
- Studies of the Letters of John & Jude
- The Tribulation to Come (A Study of Revelation)
- The Coming of the Lord Draweth Nigh
- An Overview of the Old Testament
- A Study of the Book of Job
- Studies in the Pentateuch: Genesis
- Studies in the Pentateuch: Exodus
- Studies in the Pentateuch: Leviticus
- Studies in the Pentateuch: Numbers
- Studies in the Pentateuch: Deuteronomy
- Global Climate Change, the Bible, & Science
- Absolute Truth for a Relative World
- A People of His Own — A Study of God's Will
- Angels — God's Messengers
- My Bout with Multiple Myeloma

Ceramic Books include:

- Particle Calculations for Ceramists
- Rheology for Ceramists
- Reología para Ceramistas
- Characterization Techniques for Ceramists
- Practical Pointers for Ceramists, Volumes I & II